THE
MARIAN
OPTION

THE

OPTION

God's Solution to a Civilization in Crisis

CARRIE GRESS, PhD

TAN Books
Charlotte, North Carolina

Cover design by Caroline Kiser

Library of Congress Cataloging-in-publication Data

Names: Gress, Carrie, author.
Title: The Marian option: God's solution to a civilization in crisis / Carrie Gress, PhD.
Description: Charlotte: TAN Books, 2017. |
    Includes bibliographical references.
Identifiers: LCCN 2017004254 (print) | LCCN 2017012996 (ebook) | ISBN 9781505109115 (ePub) | ISBN 9781505109122 (mobi) | ISBN 9781505109108 (hardcover)
Subjects: LCSH: Mary, Blessed Virgin, Saint.
Classification: LCC BT603 (ebook) | LCC BT603.G74 2017 (print) | DDC 232.91—dc23
LC record available at https://lccn.loc.gov/2017004254

Published in the United States by
TAN Books
P. O. Box 410487
Charlotte, NC 28241
www.TANBooks.com

Printed in the United States of America

For my own saintly Joseph

And for Catherine, Noelle, Robert, and Duncan

May you always stay close to your Mother

Every great reform begins with a return to basics—back to the rock from which we were hewn (see Is 51:1). And there is no more basic principle in our faith than to be with Our Lord in the house of Mary. With a winning combination of intellectual depth and traditional devotion, Dr. Carrie Gress lays out a way forward for our difficult time.

—Fr. Paul Scalia,
author of *That Nothing May Be Lost*

The Marian Option is a breath of fresh air. Bringing together the current cultural challenge and the beautiful presence and work of Our Lady, Dr. Gress gives us an encouraging message of hope. There are very few scholars who could so artfully display the power of Our Lady in such a consoling and compelling way. This book is a retreat, a gift, and a summons to all people of faith.

—Fr. Jeffrey F. Kirby, STD,
author of *Lord, Teach Us to Pray*

Through this beautifully written book, Dr. Carrie Gress makes the case for the importance of the role of the Mother of God in cultural renewal and the defense of Christian civilization. This book reminds us of the unique relationship of the Theotokos—the God Bearer—with her Son, providing a spark that might deepen our own participation in the worship of the Father, through her Son and in the Spirit. Through these, every Christian will be supernaturally transformed and become an active agent in the evangelization of the culture that is so needed.

—David Clayton, Pontifex University,
author of *The Way of Beauty*

CONTENTS

AUTHOR'S NOTE

The idea for this book certainly did not come in a flash of inspiration. Rather, it was the culmination of many different events. The first spark happened in an article I wrote for *Catholic World Report*, "John Paul II's Field Guide in the Battle for Religious Freedom." Shortly thereafter, I was asked by the Acton Institute to teach two classes at their annual Acton University. Intrigued by the idea of the Benedict Option, I decided to explore Rod Dreher's thoughts and contrast them to the life of Pope St. John Paul II, who witnessed decades of Christian persecution. While considering the elements of battling Christian persecution, it occurred to me that Our Lady has been the strongest force in conquering enemies, making converts, and renewing culture. It didn't take long for me to see that there was a whole lot more to the story than I realized.

As *The Marian Option* unfolded for me, I published several articles related to it in my blog posts for the *National Catholic Register*: "Meeting the Queen of Poland at Częstochowa," "Before Taking the Benedict Option, Try the Marian Option," "15 Ways to Live the Marian Option," and "The Fascinating Link Between Lepanto and Our Lady of Guadalupe." I have also included an excerpt from an article from *Aleteia*, "The 'Picturing Mary' Exhibit Brings a Different Kind of Woman to Washington, DC," in this book because it contrasts the values of the world with those of Christians.

I would particularly like to thank Carl Olson at *Catholic World Report*, Kevin Knight at the *National Catholic Register*, and Elizabeth Scalia at *Aleteia* for kindly allowing me to reprint portions of these articles in this book.

INTRODUCTION

There is a growing sense of unease in the world today. People of every political stripe and creed are concerned that the world seems to be spinning out of control. Homesteading, living off the grid, and "prepping" are trends that many have quietly been undertaking for some time, but suddenly, those who would never have considered something so radical are now contemplating packing up and moving out into the country. While the promise of a simpler life—more connected to earth, air, and sky—is part of the appeal, there's more to it than that. People are looking for something solid, concrete, reliable, safe, wholesome, and beautiful. Our secular culture and the ghastly news cycle have left many people wondering, "What should we do? How should we live our lives in the face of so much chaos?"

In the wake of September 11, *Wall Street Journal* reporter Peggy Noonan wrote about many people's deeper reflection because of that tragic day:

> There are a lot of quiet moments going on. Have you noticed? A lot of quiet transformations, a lot of quiet action and quiet conversations. People are realigning themselves. I know people who are undergoing

religious conversions, and changes of faith. And people who are holding on in a new way, with a harder grip, to what they already have and believe in.

Some people have quietly come to terms with the most soul-chilling thoughts. A young man I know said to me last week, as we chatted in passing on the street, "I have been thinking about the end of the American empire." And I thought: *Oh my boy, do you know the import, the weight, of the words you are saying?* And then I thought *Yes, he does. He's been thinking, quietly.*[1]

These are the same sort of quiet moments people are having now—but somehow, the stakes seem higher, particularly for Catholicism. Mocking and disparaging Catholicism has been called the last acceptable form of bigotry. No other group has continued to hold a strong line on life, family, and marriage—the fundamentals of any flourishing society. The Church and her members will continue to pay a price for defending the most defenseless and upholding the law written within our hearts.

The Benedict Option

The late law professor Charles Rice, during his brilliant career at Notre Dame Law School, would frequently tell his students back in the seventies, eighties, and nineties that contraception would eventually lead the

---

1   Peggy Noonan, "His Delicious, Mansard-Roofed World," *Wall Street Journal,* October 26, 2001, http://www.peggynoonan .com/158/?hilite=2001.

country to same-sex marriage. He was generally laughed off as a bit too doomsday or even half-mad because—so they thought—such a thing could never happen. Sadly, his prophecy became a reality just a few months after his death in February 2015. Same-sex marriage was made the law of the land in June 2015 through the Supreme Court ruling *Obergefell v. Hodges*, decided by the slim majority of one Supreme Court judge.

Shortly after the fateful ruling, journalist and author Rod Dreher suggested that *Obergefell* was an indication of the direction the culture was going. Christians, he argued, would be well served to consider how to respond to religious persecution and societal collapse. His warning was clear: things are bad, and they are only going to get worse. In the face of observable chaos, Dreher wonders, how can we be faithful as post-Christian America quickly turns into anti-Christian America?

Dreher offered his own suggestion about how to live under deep persecution: the Benedict Option. His idea was to follow the lead of St. Benedict (480–547 A.D.), who, as Rome was crumbling, sought refuge first as a hermit and then as an innovator of monastic life. Benedict retreated not out of fear but out of a desire to bring Christian order to a world in chaos. He is considered not only the father of monasticism but also a preserver of antiquities, many of which would have been lost if not for the monasteries he founded. Monasticism, ordered by the Rule of St. Benedict, became a place of solace in a world gone mad; hospitality, the spirit of evangelization, and deep charity reigned. The ordering of material goods, the rhythm of time, and the balance of work and prayer (*ora et labora*) not only preserved but expanded civilization at a time when the empire was left in tatters. Monasteries, through asceticism, prayer, work, and community, were also saint makers. It was through these saints that civilization was sustained and later thrived. It is this model that Dreher suggested Christians consider.

A quick look at the world around us might prompt many to agree that Dreher is on to something. Same-sex marriage is far from being the only moral battleground for Catholics: more than three thousand abortions are performed daily in the United States alone, ISIS is encroaching, Russia and China are rattling sabers as they make dramatic moves toward their neighbors, European and American borders are in disarray, and attempts are being made to combat Islamic terror through the rhetoric of hallowed-out secularism. The dizzying list makes one wonder where it will end and what rock we can hide under until it does.

So in this gathering storm of religious persecution and civilizational rot, is the Benedict Option the best path to follow? Ever since Dreher has proposed the Benedict Option, others have offered alternatives: the David Option, the Tolkien Option, the Dominican Option, and so on. In various forms, they all promote a model based on a saint (or noble figure) who has helped swing the pendulum from a hopeless time in the other direction—toward safety and/or civilizational growth. Some options require moving, some require a certain personality type, others require a particular type of vocation, and still others are not for children or the faint of heart. None, however, have a (nearly) universal application for every Catholic.

This book is not meant to be a refutation of the Benedict Option. Nor is it a refutation of the other types of options. There are great things to be said about these. It might be the case that many are called to live a type of Benedict or Dominican Option. What I am suggesting may function simultaneously with any option instead of replacing it. The goal of this book is to see that there is something more fundamental, more powerful, and more universal than these options. It is, of course, the Marian Option.

Despite only speaking six times in Scripture, the centuries have proven that Mary is one of the greatest forces in history. While many consider her to be only slightly elevated over the rest of the communion of saints, in reality, she goes far beyond every other saint in terms of who she is and her intercession for us. Being "full of grace," she is much more than we can be while providing the model for who we should be. What started out as small as a mustard seed has grown into one of the most powerful forces on earth. Mary's influence is not just acknowledged by Catholics; even the secular world has taken note. In their December 2015 issue, *National Geographic* hailed her as the "World's Most Powerful Woman," while *TIME* has called her the most revered woman in history.[2] Muslims, too, honor her because of the extensive praise of her in the Qur'an. More than just a title, she has proven over the ages that she is, in fact, the world's most powerful woman. Whether it's evangelization, stomping out heresies, or vanquishing the Church's enemies, Mary is at the heart of it all. But like a good mother, she also brings

---

2   On the cover of *TIME*, December 30, 1991, vol. 138, no. 26.

order, beauty, and peace wherever she is welcomed. We see it in the soaring heights of Chartres Cathedral, the sublime beauty of Michelangelo's *Pietà*, and the delicate touch of Botticelli's *Madonna of the Book*.

As we will see in these pages, the Marian Option offers the key to personal and societal transformation in ways that no other saint or noble leader can, precisely because of who she is—the Mother of God, our spiritual mother, and the perfect link between heaven and earth. The Marian Option is a type of spiritual "hunkering down" where we pick up our rosaries and other Marian devotions and follow the lead of the world's most powerful woman.

Finding the Real Mary

There might be many reasons we overlook or are unaware of Mary's power and efficacy. For some, the Rosary seems to simply be only for the soft-headed or those looking for Mary's image in toast or tortillas. For others, perhaps it is that the gentle handmaiden doesn't resonate with our contemporary image of what powerful women do. Or perhaps it's a challenge to see that praying a Rosary leads to real change. For some, a damaged relationship with an earthly mother can present an obstacle to trusting a heavenly one. Regardless, what we forget at our own peril is that Mary has a long and illustrious history of revealing to humanity the awesome power of her love and intercession.

One ironic hurdle to understanding Mary has come in the form of unapproved Marian apparitions. Michael O'Neill, known as the "Miracle Hunter" for his unrelenting efforts to investigate the miraculous, reports that in recent decades, there have been more than two thousand five hundred reported apparitions of Our Lady. Almost none have full approval from the Vatican, while some have received approval from local bishops. Most, however, are not and will not be approved until some time in the future—generally after the individual(s) reporting the apparition have died and the full evidence and fruit of the events can be weighed properly. While not ruling out the possibility that many of these apparitions could be authentic, the level of apparition saturation, along with rampant speculation about what they mean, has had a negative effect on many people (myself included). It seems wiser to just avoid them all because one simply cannot be sure of their authenticity. There is, however, a wealth of information about Mary to be mined from Scripture and other reliable sources, including the fifteen Vatican-approved apparitions—such as her appearances at Guadalupe, Lourdes, and Fatima—as well as the writings of canonized saints.

All these obstacles to understanding who the real Mary is have stalled the discussion about Mary's role throughout history, particularly related to her aid in our salvation, her role in creating culture, and her miraculous intercession over the ages. When considering her, it's easier to look to one event, like the Battle of Lepanto, or one apparition, like Our Lady Guadalupe, and miss the entire backstory and connection between these events. Mary has an amazing track record that only becomes more striking the deeper one looks. It is this illustrious history that *The Marian Option* will look at carefully, making it obvious for even the most casual reader that there really is something about Mary that demands our attention.

Living the Marian Option does not require a change of address, career, or nationality; what it does require is going deep in one's faith by both living the sacramental life and acknowledging Mary as our spiritual mother. Venerable Archbishop Fulton Sheen has pointed out that Mary's role is always to prepare us for Jesus.[3] Following her option requires nothing less than spiritual maturity, which ironically comes from childlike trust in her intercession, wisdom, and love.

Simple, Not Superficial

At first glance, the Marian Option might appear to be simple—perhaps too simple. The only requirement is a relationship with Our Lady. But simplicity is not the same as superficiality. Many things that seem simple can be powerful, efficacious, and surprisingly profound. Like a clear and calm lake, there can be hidden depths, despite appearances. The love between child and mother is remarkably simple, but one of the strongest bonds on earth. How much more so between the Mother given to us by Jesus at the foot of the Cross and her children? It's easy to forget that she is not only real but also eager to help us, longing to have a relationship—a deep and fruitful relationship—with each one of us. She knows better than anyone just what it cost her Son to redeem us; she doesn't want to see it squandered.

---

3   Fulton J. Sheen, *The World's First Love*, 2nd ed. (San Francisco: Ignatius Press, 2010), 190.

Why an Option?

Some have asked, "Why do we need an option, anyway? Isn't it enough to just be Catholic?" With every other option, including the Benedict Option, the answer is yes, it is enough to be Catholic, provided one is going to Mass and confession regularly, following Church teaching, and animating his or her soul with prayer. Sadly, however, few Catholics are doing these things. The Marian Option is distinct because Mary isn't simply another saint; she is the singular mode through which Christ came and comes to us. She has been given a unique role in salvation history through the Trinity. She makes this clear in her apparitions, and many a pope, saint, and Church document has reiterated this over the ages. Pope St. John Paul II explained that we are living in very unique times and facing a struggle unlike that of previous generations. He said, "We are today before the greatest combat that mankind has ever seen. I do not believe that the Christian community has completely understood it. We are today before the final struggle between the Church and the anti-Church, between the Gospel and the anti-Gospel."[4]

It is because of this struggle that we need to draw upon every resource God has offered us—particularly His Mother, who, like every good mother, knows what her children need even before they do.

The Marian Option is, in actuality, a simple idea executed through simple actions. But it's also nothing short of a road

---

4   Karol Wojtyła, speech to the American Bishops (1967; repr., *Wall Street Journal*, November 9, 1978).

map to unite ourselves with Christ in a dramatic way that can transform both our own souls and the world. Every other option is just that—optional—but as these pages will demonstrate, the Marian Option isn't an option. It is a necessity.

Part I

Mary and Creative Minorities

CHAPTER I

The Benedictine Model

Two thousand years of Christianity have supplied scores of stories about how to respond to persecution. The first response to Christian persecution took place in 1 A.D., when Mary and Joseph fled with the child Jesus to Egypt. Families who did not flee, however, had their infant sons brutally murdered by King Herod's soldiers. Still today, we honor their sacrifice, the Holy Innocents, as the first martyrs for Christ every December 28. It is fair to say that Christian persecution has been with us since the very beginning. Jesus told us to expect it (see 2 Tm 3:12), so we shouldn't be surprised to find ourselves facing it yet again.

We have thousands of examples of saints dealing with persecution—some who remained in and some who fled from their respective civilizations. In both cases, many were martyred. There are even saints who did both, such as St. Polycarp, who journeyed from farm to farm until his hiding place was finally betrayed, only to be martyred in Rome's coliseum. Or St. Teresa Benedicta of the Cross (Edith Stein), a Jewish convert who was moved to a convent in the Netherlands during World War II, only to be discovered and sent to Auschwitz, where she perished. We also have examples of those who were going to flee but then changed their minds, like the first pope, St. Peter.

But what can we learn from those who have gone before us? The most obvious answer is that there is more than one way to deal with persecution.

Christians today are facing not only persecution but also the threat of civilizational collapse. When St. Benedict of Nursia founded his first monastery, he wasn't trying to escape persecution per se. Having lived in Rome, he knew the depth of its corruption. Not only was it crumbling as a civilization, but it was shot through with paganism, making it an incredibly difficult culture to renew because every cultural symbol—every flower and cloud—carried with it some sort of association with pagan imagery. What made Roman persecutions so aggressive was that the Roman Empire lacked anything resembling Christian roots. Humility, suffering, charity, monotheism, and the Cross were a scandal to Romans and contrary to the very things the Romans believed made them a great empire.

The parallels between America today and the crumbling Roman Empire are striking and have been pointed out by historians and cultural critics for decades. It seems only natural, then, that St. Benedict, who was the civilizational savior of the post-Roman world, should be invoked for similar times. But today's situation is complicated by weapons of mass destruction, globalism, technology, drones, surveillance, and unwieldy states with bloated government regulations shaping even the most mundane details of our daily lives. As a result, a true retreat from the world and its threats seems next to impossible. Even so, it is important to consider our options.

Creative Minorities

Civilizations have a life-span. A cursory look at world history reveals this truth, from ancient Egypt and Persia, to Greece and the Roman Empire, to the British Empire, upon which the sun never set. They have all waxed and waned. As historian Arnold Toynbee (1889–1975) noted, civilizations rarely die simply from external assault; they are first hollowed out by internal moral decline. "Civilizations," Toynbee wrote, "die from suicide, not by murder."[1] They are weakened from the inside out, like an old tree rotted to the core and knocked down by the slightest wind.

Toynbee, in his exhaustive research of twenty-six great civilizations, saw that they arose not from easy situations or in places that offered the least resistance to the needs of humanity—quite the contrary. He found that it was the rough edges of resistance, persecution, and challenge that brought forth new civilizations from the ashes of the old. These emerging civilizations rose not from massive populist movements but from the virtues of small "creative minorities." According to Toynbee, these creative minorities stretch the boundaries of a crumbling empire and transform it into

---

1   Arnold Toynbee, qtd. in Samuel Gregg, "Benedict's Creative Minority," *Acton Institute* (blog), September 22, 2010, http://www.acton.org/pub/commentary/2010/09/22/benedict%E2%80%99s-creative-minority.

something new. They are "no more than a leaven in the lump of ordinary humanity."[2] The creative minority is generally led by creative individuals. Toynbee explains, "The creator, when he arises, always finds himself overwhelmingly out-numbered by the inert uncreative mass, even when he has the good fortune to enjoy the companionship of a few kin-dred spirits."[3]

Toynbee suggests two ways in which creative minorities effect a shift in culture. The first is to drill a message into the minds of the unthinking masses, perhaps through something like social media; the second is to use what Toynbee calls a mystic. This second way comes from those creative individ-uals who are able to enter the world but also exit it through prayer. In prayer, the mystic draws strength and inspiration that they then carry back to the world to transform commu-nities and culture in ways unimaginable. The mystic's retreat allows an individual to return to the world transformed and ready to transform it.

The reality that civilizations are expanded by a relative few should offer great hope to us as we watch what appears to be the crumbling of Western civilization before our very eyes. A mass movement isn't needed—only a very few who know the true source of strength, grace, and genius to trans-form the world. Among Toynbee's examples of the geniuses behind creative minorities are Moses, St. Gregory the Great (who spent three years in seclusion before establishing order

---

2   Arnold Toynbee, *A Study of History: Abridgement of Volumes I–VI*,
     ed. D. C. Somervell (New York: Oxford University Press, 1974), 215.
3   Ibid., 214.

in the Church and a peace with the barbarians), and of course, St. Benedict of Nursia, to whom we will turn next. Others have pointed out that St. Thomas More and his stand against Henry VIII was a one-man creative minority. A most obvious example of creative minority is Christ and the twelve men He chose to transform the world through the spread of Christianity.[4]

Pope Benedict XVI was a proponent of creative minorities, offering the idea as his vision for the Catholic Church's role in contemporary Europe. Pope Benedict's model of the creative minority did not suggest a full-scale retreat or ghettoization of Christians. Like Toynbee suggested, the German pope was talking not about circling the wagons and cutting oneself off from the world but about engaging the world after dowsing oneself in prayer.

St. Benedict's Model

Among the many types of creative minorities, St. Benedict's model is one that stands out. It is unique in that it has a retreating characteristic to it. Yes, it certainly can involve the building up of local community, but by its nature, it is not actively engaging an urban population directly. Through St. Benedict, monasticism eventually spread to all of Europe, transforming education, economics, theology, and the arc of history. Benedict's famous dictum—*ora et labora*, "prayer and work"—is really the embodiment of the creative minority by emphasizing both communing with God and acting in the world.

---

4   Gregg, "Benedict's Creative Minority."

Before looking closely at St. Benedict's model of dealing with Christian persecution, we first need to look at who St. Benedict was. Benedict (480–547 A.D.) was born into a wealthy noble family in Nursia, Italy, a couple hours' drive outside Rome. Raised Catholic, he had a deepening of faith when he went to study in Rome. You can still visit the church in Rome, San Benedetto in Piscinula, that is on the site of his family's palazzo in the Trastevere district of the city. This church today features a small chapel where the servants' cloakroom had been, a place Benedict used as a prayer cell.

Benedict eventually left the filth of pagan Rome and lived as a hermit in a cave in Subiaco for three years, where he was mentored by another hermit. He was then invited to lead a community of monks, which ended badly when one monk (or perhaps all) tried to poison him. Benedict went on to establish twelve monasteries with at least twelve monks in each, guided by the Benedictine Rule, which is a detailed explanation of how to live monastic life. He later established Monte Cassino—known as the most famous monastery in all of Europe. All the monasteries Benedict organized were devoted not only to their own work and prayer but also to evangelizing and taking care of the needs of local populations. This monastic system gave him the title father of monasticism even though monasteries were not a new phenomenon during his time. His monastic system is also credited with saving the remnants of Western civilization that surely would have been lost during the Dark Ages without the care of monks throughout Europe.

Why Retreat?

St. Benedict did not leave Rome for his own safety. Christian persecution had come largely to an end by this point after Constantine made Christianity the state religion of Rome with the Edict of Milan. Benedict left so he could follow Christ more completely. The long-term dry martyrdom of the ascetics replaced the violent and bloody martyrdom of the persecutions. The whole idea of Benedict's monastery was to find a way to follow Christ more closely and to engage in the battle for good and evil according to God's will. The monastery was and remains a strategic effort to save the world and souls. St. Benedict and his companions recognized that they could offer the world more by retreating from it instead of engaging in it; in other words, they retreated from the world precisely to save the world. It is in the monastery that they helped wage spiritual warfare against all that is evil—through prayer, intercession, penance, and atonement for sin. If the only reason for their founding was to save Western civilization after the collapse of Rome, then the monastic system would have ceased to be needed centuries ago. St. Benedict and every Benedictine who has followed (one prays) understood that the monastery is not a place to hide from problems; it is a place to face them, whether they are personal sin, human brokenness, persecution, or civilizational collapse. Through the ordered and penitential life of monks, the disorder of the world can be tamed, silenced, and renewed.

What St. Benedict was able to promote through the monastery system and his rule were the basic elements for building a wider community and civilization. Monasteries were able to address everything from basic human needs (food, clothing, and shelter) to the spiritual necessities (evangelization, education, common sense, hospitality, prayer, gracious manners, and self-discipline). The monasteries also jumpstarted local economies through the massive expansion of agriculture and technological innovations while affirming the value of hard work. None of this could have been done in an urban center; a remote and protected site was necessary to ward off invading barbarians and other enemies.

St. Benedict is truly a source of inspiration and hope, but the question remains: Is St. Benedict's model best suited for contemporary concerns?

A New St. Benedict?

As noted earlier, the current discussion of St. Benedict's model has been made popular by Rod Dreher in his book *The Benedict Option: A Strategy for Christians in a Post-Christian Nation* (2017).[5] Dreher says that his idea originated with philosopher Alasdair MacIntyre, best known for his book *After Virtue* (1981). In it, MacIntyre takes a pessimistic view, arguing that the Enlightenment project has failed and the West is already lost and hopelessly corrupted down to its intellectual roots. The last lines of MacIntyre's book read as follows:

> What matters at this stage is the construction of local forms of community within which civility and the

---

5   Rod Dreher, *The Benedict Option: A Strategy for Christians in a Post-Christian Nation* (New York: Sentinel, 2017).

intellectual and moral life can be sustained through the new dark ages which are already upon us. And if the tradition of the virtues was able to survive the horrors of the last dark ages, we are not entirely without grounds for hope. This time however, the barbarians are not waiting beyond the frontiers; they have already been governing us for quite some time. And it is our lack of consciousness of this that constitutes part of our predicament. We are waiting not for a Godot, but for another—doubtless very different—St. Benedict.[6]

As we have just seen, the notion of following in the footsteps of St. Benedict is very appealing, but MacIntyre says something very interesting. He says we are waiting for "another—doubtless very different—St. Benedict." MacIntyre made it clear that the St. Benedict of old didn't need to be reincarnated; rather, something or someone new was needed. While it is always difficult to conjecture what MacIntyre might mean because he is a challenging writer and thinker, looking at Christian history offers a few clues.

The first clue is to consider what St. Benedict was called to build on: the Roman Empire. While there are dramatic parallels between ancient Rome and our day, there are also a lot of differences. The first difference is the deep imprint paganism left on the Roman mind. It's hard for us to comprehend the extent to which paganism influenced how Romans perceived every natural element of the world. While most of us think of

---

6   Alasdair MacIntyre, *After Virtue*, 3rd ed. (1981; repr., South Bend: University of Notre Dame Press, 2007), 263.

the Dark Ages—those murky years of history when barbar-
ian hoards, chaos, ignorance, and superstition ruled—G. K.
Chesterton explained that this period had an altogether different reality and purpose. Of the Dark Ages, he says, "It was
the end of a penance; or, if it be preferred, a purgation. It
marked the moment when a certain spiritual expiation had
been finally worked out and certain spiritual diseases had been
finally expelled from the system. They had been expelled by
an era of asceticism, which was the only thing that could have
expelled them. Christianity had entered the world to cure the
world; and she had cured it in the only way in which it could
be cured."[7]

That cure was through amputation, so to speak. The old
Hellenic/Roman world had to be purged of its pagan associations. Chesterton explains further, "It was no metaphor to
say that these people needed a new heaven and a new earth;
for they had really defiled their own earth and even their
own heaven."[8]

One of the most essential elements that needed renewing was the Roman understanding of women and goddesses.
Venus, the central woman of Roman mythology, represented
fertility, love, sex, beauty, and victory. The ruins of temples
that honored her still dot Rome. In Roman mythology,
Venus was considered the mother of Rome, having given
birth to a son, Aeneas, who populated Italy. Julius Caesar
even claimed her as an ancestor. There would have been a

---

7   G. K. Chesterton, *The Collected Works of G. K. Chesterton*, vol. 2
      (San Francisco: Ignatius Press, 1987), 23.
8   Ibid., 40.

mental chasm for most Romans to bridge (though it was clearly not impossible, since many did so) from an understanding of a goddess—full of jealousy, manipulation, seduction, and desire—to a new Virgin Mother, who was pure and sinless. Even the Roman festival of wine held on April 23 for Venus, the goddess of profane wine—that is, wine for everyday use—would have to be scrubbed of its ancient meaning to accommodate Mary as the mother of the God who offers us Sacred Wine.

Christianity offered a new way to see nature and to know God, but before this vision could be accepted en masse, paganism had to be eliminated. "How could their case be met by looking at the sky," Chesterton asks, "when erotic legends were scrawled in stars across it; how could they learn anything from the love of birds and flowers after the sort of love stories that were told of them?"[9] He continues, "Nothing could purge this obsession but a religion that was literally unearthly. It was no good telling such people to have a natural religion full of stars and flowers; there was not a flower or even a star that had not been stained. They had to go into the desert where they could find no flowers or even into the cavern where they could see no stars. Into that desert and that cavern the highest human intellect entered for some four centuries; and it was the very wisest thing it could do."[10]

As Chesterton makes clear, it is no accident that the Desert Fathers of the Church were in the desert wastelands during

---

9   Ibid.
10   Ibid.

this time, where Benedict's protected monasteries were free of pagan influence. This was not the case in the cities, where persecution persisted up until the year 313 (though martyrdom provided much Christian fruit in the cities). It's easy to see how St. Benedict's retreat was an integral part of this period of purification. People had to relearn how to see the world, and that is difficult to do when the eyes have already been corrupted. The cleaning process, or the penance, came to an end as the Dark Ages drew to a close. "Men at the close of the Dark Ages may have been rude and unlettered and unlearned in everything but wars with heathen tribes," Chesterton adds, "but they were clean. They were like children; the first beginnings of their rude arts have all the clean pleasure of children."[11] Interestingly, it is at this stage—after the deep cleaning—that the creative minorities of St. Norbert, St. Bernard, St. Francis, and St. Dominic enter the scene (along with a "little thing" called the Rosary), helping usher in a full bloom of culture.

St. Benedict was vital in terms of offering not just succor but real civilizational growth to the West, allowing Christianity to sink its roots deeply into time and space. And while devotion to Our Lady was on the rise—she was already considered the New Eve by the Desert Fathers, proclaimed Mother of God by the Church, and revered deeply by St. Benedict and his monks—a fuller devotion to her would unfold over time, opening the door to a different type of creative minority whose power is, even today, largely unknown or underestimated.

---

11   Ibid., 41.

Real Takeaway: Hope and Prayer

Examining the different creative minorities provides hope that a few simple souls can make a difference in the world. And after skimming salvation history, it is also comforting to know that there are manifold ways to be a creative minority. Many might be called to something like the Benedict Option, but it is certainly not for everyone, given the natural obstacles of considering a move to a remote location. Moreover, it should not be seen as a "safe" alternative, where those who engage in it can avoid the Cross. Retreat is certainly no guarantee that one will survive or avoid persecution and struggle.

The vital takeaway for understanding creative minorities is to see the critical importance of prayer. There is much that is good about St. Benedict's model and the Benedict Option, but like MacIntyre, I think there is a better alternative. We will look to that next.

CHAPTER 2

The Most Powerful
Woman in the World

When in Italy, if you ask the name of a relatively unknown church, the response is likely *Santa Maria della Qualcosa*, or "St. Mary of Something," testifying to the number of churches in Italy named after Our Lady. It seems that every little town—from Seville to St. Petersburg and every pocket of Catholicism in between—has at least one, if not several, churches devoted to Our Lady. Rome alone has roughly ninety. Many are filled with votive or thanksgiving offerings testifying to the prayers answered through Mary's intercession, among them crutches, glasses, photographs, and paintings.

In 1900, Henry Adams (1838–1918), grandson of President John Quincy Adams and great-grandson of President John Adams, had a keen insight. In his work *The Education of Henry Adams*,[1] he explains the wonder and ignorance he felt

---

1   Henry Adams, *The Education of Henry Adams* (New York: Literary Classics of the United States, Library of America, 1983).

as a young man at the World's Fair while experiencing the power of new machines, especially the automobile. While he found himself stupefied by the invention, he was thrilled by its potential and what it heralded for the future of science. But then Adams retreats a bit from his awe and wonder and compares the likes of it to the power wielded throughout the centuries by the notion of a virgin. He starts initially describing those found among the Greeks and Romans, but eventually his descriptions include the Virgin Mary. He explains, "The twelfth and thirteenth centuries were a period when men were at their strongest; never before or since have they shown equal energy in such varied directions, or such intelligence in the direction of their energy; yet these marvels of history—these Plantegenets [a dynastic family of kings]; these Scholastic philosophers; these architects of Rheims and Amiens; these Innocents, and Robin Hoods, and Marco Polos; these crusaders who planted their enormous fortresses all over the Levant; these monks who made the wastes and barrens yield harvest—all, without apparent expedition, bowed down before the woman."[2]

Even the potential power of the dynamo (the automobile) is nothing, Adams explains, compared to the power of the Virgin. What Henry Adams recognized more than a century ago (even more surprisingly as a Protestant) as he walked through the cities, churches, cathedrals, and cemeteries, was that the height of European culture was centered on devotion to Our Lady. In the places where European culture

---

2   Henry Adams, *Mont St. Michel and Chartres* (New York: Literary Classics of the United States, Library of America, 1983), 568.

soared, so too did devotion to Our Lady, and perhaps vice versa: where devotion to Mary soared, so too did culture.

Henry Adams isn't the only one to have this insight about Mary. In 2015, *National Geographic* named her the "World's Most Powerful Woman." Maureen Orth explained:

> Mary is everywhere: Marigolds are named for her. Hail Mary passes save football games. The image in Mexico of Our Lady of Guadalupe is one of the most reproduced female likenesses ever. Mary draws millions each year to shrines such as Fatima, in Portugal, and Knock, in Ireland, sustaining religious tourism estimated to be worth billions of dollars a year and providing thousands of jobs. She inspired the creation of many great works of art and architecture (Michelangelo's "Pietà," Notre Dame Cathedral), as well as poetry, liturgy, and music (Monteverdi's *Vespers for the Blessed Virgin*). And she is the spiritual confidante of billions of people, no matter how isolated or forgotten.[3]

Mary *is* everywhere—sometimes hiding in plain sight. Her influence in the world is unmistakable if looked at collectively through salvation history.

In the previous chapter, we saw that creative minorities are responsible for setting the wheels of civilizations aright. What has been overlooked for centuries, however, is Mary's role in creative minorities. Not only did she play a role in

---

3   Maureen Orth, "How the Virgin Mary Became the World's Most Powerful Woman," *National Geographic*, December 8, 2015, http://ngm.nationalgeographic.com/2015/12/virgin-mary-text.

them, but she has been the force behind some of the most successful creative minorities in history. Looking back to when devotion to her expanded in the Church—say, from the thirteenth century, when St. Dominic promoted the Rosary (although one could argue even earlier)—Mary has been the source behind the Catholic creative minorities that have ushered in massive geopolitical shifts. In battle after battle against Christianity's enemies, those led by her have been victorious. For example, Catholic Spain, fighting under her standard, is one of the only countries to regain vast amounts of territory from Islam. Elsewhere, outnumbered Christians were victorious against the Ottomans in the battles of Lepanto and Vienna after begging for Mary's assistance through the Rosary. In the Americas, Our Lady of Guadalupe dramatically transformed the history of the continent by converting at least four million natives to Catholicism (some estimates are as high as ten million). And in Cold War Poland, a priest of little consequence was called from the ashes of World War II and Soviet Communism to conquer the Iron Curtain. In country after country, from Austria to Ukraine, some national miracle has been attributed to her intercession.

Mary is truly at the heart of many creative minorities that have transformed the world. She doesn't need the masses to change; she just needs a few devoted souls, such as St. Dominic, St. Ferdinand III, Blessed Alan de la Roche, Jan Sobieski, St. Catherine Labouré, three children in Fatima, or Pope St. John Paul II. She also works through the hidden souls known only to her, who transform the world through their prayers, sacrifices, and pure love. Cardinal

Joseph Mindszenty (1892–1975), who was imprisoned first
by the Nazis and then by the Communists in Hungary for
twenty-three years, said of her, "Veneration of Mary is the
great genius which gives Christianity its power, courage, and
victoriousness."[4] Clearly this was a man who had witnessed
a lot of cowardice, injustice, and outright evil. He knew that
Mary and her special intercession was an antidote to all of
these.

The Woman in Combat Boots

Many years ago, I heard a priest with a strong Marian devotion explain that Mary wears combat boots. It seemed an
odd thing to say about the woman who is always described
as exceedingly beautiful, clothed in gorgeous flowing silks
and veils. And yet, if you look deeper at Mary's influence
over the centuries, the idea of her wearing combat boots
looks a little more plausible.

Of the many foreshadowings of Mary found in the Old
Testament, this one rings true of a beautiful woman in boots:
"Who is she that cometh forth as the morning rising, fair as
the moon, bright as the sun, terrible as an army set in array?"
(Sg 6:10).[5] She has been called *la Conquistadora*, meaning
"the conqueror" (hardly a tender title)—a popular devotion
that continues in the American Southwest. In the Litany of
Our Lady of Sorrows, her more militant side shines through.

---

4   Joseph Mindszenty, *The Face of the Heavenly Mother* (New York:
       Philosophical Library, 1951), 85.
5   Douay-Rheims Bible translation (Charlotte, NC: Saint Benedict
       Press, 2000).

In it, she is called Shield of the oppressed, Conqueror of the incredulous, Protectress of those who fight, Haven of the shipwrecked, Calmer of tempests, Retreat of those who groan, Terror of the treacherous, and Standard-bearer of the Martyrs.[6] Like a fierce mama bear, there is nothing light-weight about her intercession and protection of those devoted to her. More recently, St. Maximilian Kolbe's "Militia of the Immaculate Conception" and the Blue Army—in contrast to the Communist Red Army, formed in response to the apparitions of Fatima—also reflect her role as the twelve-star general leading her troops in a spiritual battle. One twelfth-century knight wrote, "Our Lady is powerful in battles . . . She is the hope of . . . knights who fight . . . Without her aid, knights cannot win."[7]

In the military battles where she is invoked, the scale is tipped in surprising ways for her warriors. In battle after battle, a similar storyline presents itself: The Christians are outnumbered, but they've done their spiritual homework. The fighting starts, and out of the blue, something odd happens that leads the Christians to victory. In the 1815 Battle of New Orleans during the War of 1812, General Andrew Jackson's army of six thousand faced fifteen thousand British. The residents of New Orleans joined the Ursuline nuns in praying to Our Lady of Prompt Succor. On the morning of the battle, Mass was offered at the altar, where the statue

---

6   Pope Pius VII, "Litany of Our Lady of Seven Sorrows," *EWTN*, https://www.ewtn.com/faith/teachings/maryd6g.htm.

7   Ramon Llull, *Libre de Sancta Maria* (1290), qtd. in Amy G. Remensnyder, *La Conquistadora* (London: Oxford University Press, 2014), 15.

of Our Lady of Prompt Succor had been placed, which was close enough that cannon fire could be heard in the chapel. At the very moment of Holy Communion, a courier came to the Ursuline nuns with the news that the Americans had won. The British, who had been counting on advancing under the cover of fog, were exposed and routed when the mist unexpectedly lifted at the very moment the Mass was offered. The British lost two thousand soldiers, while the Americans lost seventy-one. President James Monroe later praised General Jackson, saying, "History records no example of so glorious a victory obtained with so little bloodshed on the part of the victorious."[8] Years later, whenever Andrew Jackson visited New Orleans, he made a point of visiting the Ursuline Convent.

Similarly, during the Polish-Soviet War in the summer of 1920, during the Battle of Warsaw, it appeared that the Soviets would have an easy time defeating the disorganized Poles. Then on August 15—which would become the date of the Feast of Our Lady's Assumption—as the Russian army was approaching the Vistula River, an image of the Our Lady of Częstochowa was seen in the clouds over the river, terrifying the atheistic Bolsheviks. Following a series of battles, the Red Army was defeated in what is known today as the "Miracle on the Vistula," which halted the spread of Communism into Western Europe.

And again, in 1986 in the Philippines, the twenty-year dictatorship of Ferdinand Marcos was shaken up by the

8   "Battle of New Orleans," *History.com*, http://www.history.com/topics/battle-of-new-orleans.

election of Corazon "Cory" Aquino. But as the Marcos regime came to an end, it appeared the dictator would not go out without a fight. He sent out his loyalist military, including tanks and soldiers, to keep a grip on the country through any means possible; Marcos had given orders to fire on the people if necessary. Cardinal Jaime Sin recounts the turn of events:

> What I am telling you now was told to me by many of these same soldiers who were ready to fire on the people. The tanks were trying to penetrate the crowd. And the people were praying and showing their rosaries. That is when, according to these soldiers, the Marines who were riding on top of the tanks, the so-called Loyalists (to Marcos), they saw up in the clouds the form of the cross . . . Then, a beautiful lady appeared to them. I don't know if she appeared in the sky or was standing down on the ground. (Others would later tell me they thought she was a nun, dressed in blue, and that she was standing in front of the tanks.) So beautiful she was, and her eyes were sparkling. And the beautiful lady spoke to them like this: "Dear soldiers, stop! Do not proceed! Do not harm my children!" And when they heard that, the soldiers put down everything. They came down from the tanks and they joined the people. So, that was the end of the Loyalists.
>
> I don't know who these soldiers are. All I know is that they came here crying to me. They did not tell me that it was the Virgin. They told me only that it was a beautiful sister. But you know, (he paused, laughing heartily), I

have seen all the sisters in Manila, and there are no beautiful ones. So it must have been the Virgin![9]

Reports say there were more than one million Filipino
men, women, and children praying together in the streets,
holding their rosaries as the soldiers advanced. The Marcos
regime ended without massive bloodshed, thwarted at the
last minute by the faith-filled prayers of a million people and
the woman who wears combat boots.

Queen of Peace

Mary's strength is not just military or political. At its heart,
her influence is always directed to the will of Christ and
the salvation of sinners, but with a maternal touch. Like a
good mother, she brings peace to those in difficult situations. When Our Lady appeared to St. Catherine Labouré,
Mary told her that France would undergo terrible political
struggles for forty years, and the whole world would be in
sadness. "The moment will come," Mary explained to Catherine, "when the danger will be enormous; it will seem that
all is lost; at that moment, I will be with you; have confidence."[10] And just as Mary said, there were forty years of
political upheaval and religious persecution both in France
and elsewhere. Wars continued, including the Civil War

---

9   Pani Rose, "Cardinal Sin and the Philippine Miracle," *Byzantine
     Forum* (blog), June 22, 2005, http://www.byzcath.org/forums/
     ubbthreads.php/topics/4387/Re_Cardinal_Sin_and_the_Philli.

10   Joseph Dirvin, *Saint Catherine Labouré of the Miraculous Medal*
     (Charlotte, NC: TAN Books, 1984), http://www.ewtn.com/
     library/MARY/CATLABOU.HTM.

in the United States and the Prussian invasion of France. The darkest hour for St. Catherine and France foretold by Mary was the Paris Commune in 1871. The raging Communists sieged Paris through bloody street fighting, desecrating churches and tombs of saints. Even the archbishop was assassinated. When the Communist ruffians took over part of St. Catherine's convent, the nuns were forced to scatter to other convents to protect themselves against the drunken mob of rapacious men. The forewarnings Mary gave to St. Catherine, however, gave her an unflappable calm, even at the darkest moments. As we will see in later chapters, saint after saint speaks of the peace, consolation, and confidence that Our Lady instilled in their hearts—no matter how grave the circumstances.

Mary has shown herself as a mother and the Queen of Peace the world over. There are apparition sites dotting the planet. A visit to the National Shrine of the Immaculate Conception in Washington, DC, makes Mary's connection to the nations of the world abundantly clear, with its seventy chapels dedicated to the Blessed Mother's international influence, from China to Africa, from Austria to Vietnam. So many countries (Catholic *and* non-Catholic) have been on the receiving end of her great graces and now feature shrines to her that are sources of grace, blessing, and peace. They remind us of the words of St. Peter Damian, who said that Mary is "the Mother of true Peace."

Beyond the Battlefield

When most battles are concluded, military personnel move on to another battle. Mary's influence, however, doesn't stop

at routing enemies; it extends into transforming the landscape. She fortifies the community and country through the
workings of culture.

As we saw in the previous chapter, in the order of history
(though not in the order of grace), Our Lady's more tangible influence in the world followed that of St. Benedict. He
brought order and stability to monasteries and the societies
that grew up around them. There was an essential scouring of
all things pagan, a belief system that had proliferated under
the Roman Empire. The Dark Ages cleaned nature and cre-
ation in the collective minds of Western civilization of pagan
associations and left the world anew again, like pure soil in
which culture and society could finally take root and grow
properly. This is not to say that these societies were without
sin or scoundrels but that there was a fundamental understanding among men and women of who God was and their
relationship to Him. From this strong starting point—like a
sturdy foundation—culture could be built. It is no accident
that devotion to Our Lady increased dramatically after the
scouring of paganism.

Looking at history, cultures are transformed through simple devotion to her. A wise priest once defined culture as
"God's love made visible." Mary is the masterpiece of God,
which explains why when Marian devotion flourishes, so
too does culture. Mary as our mother brings order to those
places where she is invoked and honored. As Blessed John
Henry Cardinal Newman, a convert from Anglicanism to
Catholicism, explained, Mary is our "happier world." She
leads her spiritual children to her Son and helps us regain
what has been lost through the Fall and sin. She rids us of

false teaching. Far from a saccharine devotion, Mary burns through the vices of the cynic, the jaded, the angry, the agitated, and the hopeless. In their place, she plants the gifts of peace, order, hope, strength, goodness, and creativity. These new fruits in the lives of her devotees become tangible in the material elements of the culture. Her gifts ripple from one person to the next well out into the broader culture.

Chapter 3

Mary, Cultivator of Culture

A couple years ago, I went to an art exhibit in Washington, DC, at the National Museum of Women in the Arts. They had a new exhibit on Marian art that featured sixty-eight incredible pieces on loan from the Vatican museums, the Louvre in Paris, and the Uffizi Gallery in Florence, Italy. The artists included such greats as Botticelli, Caravaggio, Gentileschi, and Michelangelo.

With my three-month-old baby in tow, I wondered as I drove to the museum if there would be a good place to nurse. "Of course, it's a women's museum," I assured myself.

After purchasing my ticket for the exhibit, I asked where I might nurse my son. "We have a big bathroom on the second floor, but there's nowhere to sit there," replied the museum guide.

"Don't you think it's a bit ironic that this is a museum about women, but you don't have a place for a mother to nurse her child?"

"Hmm, well . . . there's a wheelchair in the cloak closet you could use."

Despite this attempt at being helpful, I ended up going to a nearby hotel lobby when it was time to nurse my son. Clearly, I was not the museum's regular clientele. This contrast between women who have done things like nurse their children since the beginning of time and women straining for power and influence in the nation's capital was a continual theme of my visit. It is hard to imagine a deeper divide in the understanding of womanhood than the cutthroat culture of Washington as compared to the type of woman depicted in all those paintings. And yet, nestled in the center of the five-story building in the very heart of Washington, DC, was a hidden sanctuary offering visions of a woman who, in her silence, drowns out the shrill individualism toward which the rest of the city is lunging. Only Mary could find a way to penetrate what seems impenetrable.

But Mary's admittance to the women's museum was not because she was meek, humble, or a fitting model of the twenty-first-century woman—far from it—but because these sixty-eight works of art represented the heights of culture to which even the most secular among us still give homage. So how is it that this young woman from Nazareth—so contrary to modern manners—has influenced and is still influencing culture?

Mary the Masterpiece

Dating back to the earliest stages of Church history, beginning with St. Irenaeus in the third century, Mary has been called the New Eve; with her fiat, she changed everything. She is the end of the old law and the start of the new covenant with God. As one theologian has written, "She embodies a new beginning of God's covenant with humanity. In her existence, the original concept of human being is reinstated . . . [She marks] the humble beginning of the Christian era and its utter dependence on the Spirit's fire and light at Pentecost."[1] It is in this new order of the Holy Spirit that her impressions and her influence are easiest to see: "As *masterpiece*, Mary is a direct reference to the divine *artifex*: she is part of the creative manifestation of God's marvelous deeds."[2] Mariologist Father Johann Roten says that "Mary's beauty is beauty of promise and hope."[3] Marian culture, then, as an extension of Mary's virtues, isn't art for art's sake, or beauty for beauty's sake. Like Mary, it points to something—or, in this case, someone—beyond itself. To see the material elements of Marian culture, such as art, music, architecture, and literature, the viewer doesn't simply bask in its beauty or cleverness for its own sake but enters into the story of Christ. The images and forms conjure up in the viewer's memory a piece of the story, or maybe even an expansive recollection of Christ's life. And for much of Marian art, such as stained-glass windows or Stations of the Cross, the goal was truly to instruct the faithful about the life of Christ.

Noted art historian Sir Kenneth Clark stated that there is something unusual about the feminine element in religion and culture. He says, "The all-male religions (a reference to

---

1   Johann G. Roten, "Mary and the Way of Beauty," *Marian Studies* 49 (1998): 111, http://ecommons.udayton.edu/marian_studies/vol49/iss1/10.

2   Ibid.

3   Ibid.

Israel, Islam, and the Protestant North) have produced no religious imagery—in most cases have positively forbidden it. The great religious art of the world is deeply involved in the female principle."[4] With that in mind, we are reminded once again of the critical role Mary does and has played in culture over the last two thousand years, because there simply have not been other women who offer a universal "female principle" as suggested by Sir Clark.

Mary's Fingerprints

The most significant era where her fingerprints have been left is medieval Europe. The word *medieval* today has many negative connotations; if something is medieval, it's backward, crude, superstitious, and/or illogical. Most of this stems from modern faith in science and technology, which have mistakenly become the signs of progress and human achievement. While certainly we have much to be grateful for in regards to science and technology, Christians know that true faith isn't in laws of nature but in the Lawgiver; it isn't in the created but in the Creator. And no matter how rustic and backward medieval culture might be to some, there is much to be said about it and learned from it.

Philosophy

Medieval culture has the most to offer modernity in the realm of philosophy. The rigor, the tight arguments, and the demanding intellectual climate—like flint sharpening

---

4   Kenneth Clark, "Civilization," DVD Series, BBC Production, 2006.

flint—resulted in mental giants who are head and shoulders above the rest of Western civilization. During the scholastic era, under the guidance of Our Lady Seat of Wisdom, Marian devotion flourished in the work of St. Albert the Great, St. Thomas Aquinas, St. Bonaventure, and Blessed Duns Scotus. In addition to their erudite treatises—which have been influencing theology, philosophy, and law ever since—these scholars emphasized the importance of Mary. St. Thomas Aquinas (1225–74) said that the Blessed Virgin Mary "must be shown every honor, preached and praised, and invoked by us in our every need."[5] Showing a more pastoral side, St. Thomas suggested, "For in every danger you can obtain salvation from this glorious Virgin," and in every difficulty or "work of virtue you can have Mary as your helper [for] she truly says of herself, 'I am the Mother of fair love, and of fear, and of knowledge, and of holy hope, in me is all grace of the way; in me is all hope of life and of virtue' (Eccles 24:24–25)."[6]

St. Bonaventure (1217–74) offered similar praise, along with deep theological reflections. He wrote, "The Creator of all things rests in the tabernacle of the virginal womb, because here he has prepared his bridal chamber in order to become our brother; here he sets up a royal throne to become our prince; here he puts on priestly vestments to become our high priest. Because of this marital union, she is the Mother of

---

5   Mary McBride, "Prayer to Mary by Saint Thomas Aquinas," *International Marian Research Institute*, September 3, 2009, https://udayton.edu/imri/mary/p/prayer-to-mary-by-saint-thomas-aquinas.php.

6   Ibid.

God; because of the royal throne, she is the Queen of heaven; because of the priestly vestments, she is the advocate of the human race."[7] As Bonaventure makes clear, every grace from the Son first came through the Virgin's womb.

And Blessed Duns Scotus (1265–1308) can't be neglected given that out of all the conjectures about how Mary remained immaculately conceived—without the stain of original sin—he offered the most theologically compelling insight: "Just as others needed Christ, so that through his merits they might receive the forgiveness of sin already contracted, so she needs the Mediator to preserve her from sin."[8] However, as Scotus goes on to explain, the merits of the Mediator (Christ) were applied to Mary outside of time, and therefore before Christ's crucifixion took place.

St. Albert the Great (1200–80), a Dominican priest, bishop, and founder of the University of Cologne, "wrote of Mary so abundantly that there is no book written by him in which his beloved is forgotten."[9] Even his intellectual gifts were attributed to his great devotion to Mary. She gave him a mind that would serve him throughout his bright career until his last years, when his mind lost its brilliance. It resumed its brightness only once, when he needed to defend his most famous pupil, St. Thomas Aquinas, against the accusation of heresy.

---

7   Luigi Gambero, *Mary in the Middle Ages* (San Francisco: Ignatius Press, 2005), 209.
8   Ibid., 250.
9   Ibid., 222.

Just prior to the scholastic age was the Golden Age of Mary, when the study of Mary (Mariology) excelled. One of her most ardent defenders was St. Bernard of Clairvaux (1090–1158), who wrote the following:

> And the virgin's name was "Mary" (LK 1:27). Let us also say a few words about this name which means "star of the sea" and is most suitably fitting for a virgin mother. For she is most appropriately compared to a star, because, just as a star emits rays without being corrupted, so the Virgin gave birth to her Son without any injury.
>
> If you follow her, you will not go astray. If you pray to her, you will not despair. If you think of her, you will not be lost. If you cling to her, you will not fall. If she protects you, you will not fear; if she is your guide, you will not tire; if she is favorable to you, you will reach your goal. Thus you will experience personally how rightly it was spoke: "And the Virgins' name was Mary."[10]

Through men such as St. Bernard, St. Albert, and St. Thomas, Mary has also been known as the Destroyer of Heresies. She was given this title by Pope Pius X in his 1907 encyclical *Pascendi Dominici Gregis*, which spoke out against modernism—what Pius called the "synthesis of all heresies."[11] "But *how*? How does she destroy heresies?" Father Paul Scalia

---

10   Ibid., 140.

11   Pope Pius X, *Pascendi Dominici Gregis*, September 8, 1907, #58, *The Holy See*, http://w2.vatican.va/content/pius-x/en/encyclicals/documents/hf_p-x_enc_19070908_pascendi-dominici-gregis.html.

asks. "Mary never preached a sermon against error," he continues. "She never conducted an inquisition or excommunicated anyone. She never (God forbid) presented a paper at a theological conference."[12] She does it, Father Scalia explains, by inspiring zeal: "In one of those beautiful Catholic paradoxes, these men became fierce defenders of the faith by first becoming childlike towards her. Devotion to her brings purity to the soul and therefore clarity to the mind."[13] It is Mary who weeds out the untruths; it is she who combats the lies of "that ancient serpent, who is called the Devil and Satan, the deceiver of the whole world" (Rv 12:9). Like the pillar of fire that directed the journey of those carrying the Ark of the Covenant, Our Lady, the new pillar, is ever the sure guide for those who wish to avoid error.

Our Lady of the Arts

Mary's influence on painting and sculpture is perhaps the most obvious among the arts. So many artists—Michelangelo, Botticelli, Fra Angelico, and Da Vinci, to name just a few—have depicted her in the biblical stories of her life with Christ, giving viewers a new way to look at her while drawing a deeper understanding of the scriptural story. Her story and that of her Son are told in windows, frescos, altar pieces, vestments, woodcarvings, and every other medium imaginable to communicate the greatness of the gospel story.

---

12 Paul Scalia, "Mary, Destroyer of All Heresies," *The Catholic Thing*, August 4, 2016, https://www.thecatholicthing .org/2016/08/14/mary-destroyer-of-all-heresies.

13 Ibid.

Then there are the miraculous images, often anonymous, including countless icons, such as Our Lady of Kazan, or those attributed to St. Luke, such as the image of Our Lady of Częstochowa, the Vladimir Icon of the Mother of God, and the Spanish Our Lady of Guadalupe. The best-known image of Our Lady was one she designed herself as she arranged the roses in Juan Diego's tilma during the apparitions of Our Lady of Guadalupe in Mexico.

Theologian Father Roten has explained that Marian influences in culture, particularly in the form of art or icons, aren't just about evoking something delightful in the soul or pleasing to the eye. It goes much deeper. She bridges heaven and earth by helping humanity both enter into the sacred and connect with her Son. Father Roten points out that sometimes, the miraculous images of her are not aesthetically pleasing, but even so, there is something in them that draws us nearer. They create "something that is trans-visual"—that is, something that goes beyond our sense of vision, evoking something deeper in the soul.[14] It is this experience that draws pilgrims far and wide to these images, often evoking strong emotional responses, such as deep reverence, tears of sadness or joy, peace, relief, or gratitude (and sometimes all of the above).

Miraculous images, Father Roten explains, also have a communal aspect: "Images bring people together, bonding without coaxing them into uniformity. In a special way, the powerful and evocative miraculous images of Mary overcome natural divergences; they stress common ground and

---

14   Roten, "Mary and the Way of Beauty," 116.

shared destiny."[15] We can see this characteristic at work both at pilgrimage sites—like Our Lady of Częstochowa, where the image is the guardian of Poland's collective religious memory—and at places like Lourdes, where people come from all over the world and feel connected by a common bond.

Architecture

Author Stephen White wrote about what living in the shadow of a monastery dedicated to Mary meant to him:

> For miles in every direction, the tallest structures are water towers, barns, and grain silos. And then there are these spires, rising from the highest hill in that part of the state. You can't look at it without looking up. The sight of those spires, bathed in the glow of a late summer afternoon, is one of the images that shaped my imagination as a kid and changed it forever. This scene became one of the very "forms" of my own mind. It was my Minas Tirith and my Redwall Abbey. It was towers of Zion and Cair Paravel. It was every European cathedral and castle I had never seen with my own eyes. This place—Our Lady's shrine—helped keep my world enchanted and I thank God for that.[16]

---

15   Johann G. Roten, "Marian Devotion for the New Millennium," *Marian Studies* 51 (2000): 88, http://ecommons.udayton.edu/marian_studies/vol51/iss1/7.

16   Stephen P. White, personal reflection shared on Facebook.

Much of the appeal of visiting Europe is seeing its architectural crown jewels—its churches. Among them are the countless cathedrals, churches, and chapels named after the Blessed Virgin Mary. "The master-builders of all centuries," Cardinal Mindszenty explained, "were eager to fashion worthy dwellings on earth for the Queen of Heaven."[17] The efforts of these master builders speak to us still today.

One of the highest points of culture was medieval France. It is there that we find Gothic cathedrals with their flying buttresses, rose windows, soaring ceilings, and fantastic play of light and color. The master builders of the age were keen on finding the best of innovations to honor Our Lady. While at the time it was called the "New Style," what we know today as "Gothic" was a phenomenon of building that spanned two centuries, with its influences spreading near and far. Concentrated mainly in France and England, within the space of thirty-five years, eight cathedrals were under construction—usually taking more than a century to complete. The master crafters and builders who started their projects knew that they would never live to see them completed. Like a mother who will never see the complete unfolding of her work in the lives of her children and grandchildren, these men gave of themselves for future generations. Among the many Gothic churches built, roughly half of them were named after the Virgin Mary, with the best known—the French cathedrals—bearing the name *Notre Dame* ("Our Lady") in Paris, Chartres, Amiens, and Reims.

---

17   Joseph Mindszenty, *Face of the Heavenly Mother* (New York: Philosophical Library, 1951), 70.

Music

Other than Christ Himself, Mary's influence on music is unparalleled. The Second Vatican Council document *Sacrosanctum Concilum: The Constitution on the Sacred Liturgy*, issued in 1963, explains how trenchant Marian music is: "When we examine this 'treasure' [of sacred music], we discover that the Blessed Virgin Mary occupies an extraordinary place in it. In fact, through the centuries, a large number of composers have been drawn to the Mother of God, and they have dedicated to her some of their more inspired works. The quantity of these works is so great that it is impossible to give a complete list of them; the quality of many of them is such that they can rank among the best music ever written."[18]

Out of the top 154 composers in history, 117 composed pieces about the Blessed Mother, including antiphons, hymns, canticles, and sequences.[19] Among these composers, several stand out because of their particular devotion to Our Lady.

Giovanni Pierluigi Palestrina (1525–94), known as one of the princes of music, "wrote his *Stabat Mater* for eight voices and his Assumption-Mass for six voices with profound

---

18 Pope Paul VI, *Sacrosanctum Concilium*, December 4, 1963, #114, *The Holy See*, http://www.vatican.va/archive/hist_councils/ ii_vatican_council/documents/vat-ii_const_19631204 _sacrosanctum-concilium_en.html.

19 Deyanira Flores, "Lexicon of Marian Art Music" (compiled for the Marian Library/International Marian Research Institute), https://udayton.edu/imri/mary/l/lexicon-of-marian-art-music .php, table 1.

faith in a time of domestic misfortune."[20] Josef Hayden (1732–1809)—also known as Papa Hayden because he was Mozart's mentor—prayed the Rosary daily. He held onto his sacred beads when he wrote his celebrated *Stabat Mater*. Not as well known is the work of Heinrich Ignaz Franz Biber, who wrote a series of Rosary sonatas in the 1670s or 1680s. Unlike most other violin music, Biber used an unconventional type of tuning of the instruments strings; each of the fifteen sonatas that represented the mysteries of the Rosary had a different tuning that allowed them to reflect more deeply the intense joys, sorrows, and glories in the lives of Mary and Jesus.

Literature, Poetry, and Beyond

There is a tremendous amount of poetry that has been written for the Virgin Mary. Much of the poetry is in Latin, while other works were written in vernacular so the common people could understand it. Even the Nordic countries such as Norway and Sweden have expansive collections of Marian poetry written prior to the Protestant Reformation. Dante, Petrarch, Shakespeare, and Hawthorne have all featured Mary in their work. J. R. R. Tolkien said, "All my own small perception of beauty both in majesty and simplicity is founded upon Our Lady."

Among the miscellaneous elements of culture that bear Mary's influence are Mary Gardens, which are cultivated solely with plants named after her. National museums are filled with jewelry inscribed in honor of Mary. Even time has

---

20   Mindszenty, *Face of the Heavenly Mother*, 71.

been changed because of her in terms of the feasts and solem-
nities in the liturgical calendar: the current Church calendar
features thirty-two feasts attributed to her, the entire months
of May and October are devoted to her or the Rosary, and
nearly every Saturday is dedicated to Mary, a practice that
dates back at least to Pope Adrian in the eighth century.

Among all the accolades, remembrances, and feasts,
the critical element of love from the human heart must
be engaged in Marian culture. Pope Pius X explained that
the essential quality of love and devotion must be at the
center of these cultural expressions of Marian devotion.
He wrote, "Let then crowds fill the churches—let solemn
feasts be celebrated and public rejoicings be made: these are
things eminently suited for enlivening our faith. But unless
heart and will be added, they will all be empty forms, mere
appearances of piety. At such a spectacle, the Virgin, bor-
rowing the words of Jesus Christ, would address us with the
just reproach: 'This people honoureth me with their lips, but
their heart is far from me' (*Matt.* xv., 8)."[21]

No discussion of Marian culture would be complete
without the marks of justice and charity, which fun-
damentally engage the human heart. Hospitality and
caring for the most innocent—including the elderly
and orphaned—are expressions of love that honor Our
Lady. A historical "snapshot" of this can be seen in the

---

21   Pope Pius X, *Ad Diem Illum Laetissimum*, February 2, 1904,
      #16, *The Holy See*, http://w2.vatican.va/content/pius-x/en/
      encyclicals/documents/hf_p-x_enc_02021904_ad-diem
      -illum-laetissimum.html.

fifteenth-century building in Florence designed by Filippo Brunelleschi, who also designed the famous dome on the cathedral in town. While today the building is a museum, the gallery of the Ospedale degli Innocenti ("Hospital of the Innocent") was originally made for the city's most helpless: orphaned children. The orphanage's church was called Santa Maria degli Innocenti ("Our Lady of the Innocents") and featured artwork by the city's most talented artists of the day, including a painting by Domenico di Michelino that shows Mary holding her cloak around children of all ages who lived at the orphanage. It's hard to imagine other ages enlisting their best architects and painters to depict this love for abandoned children.

Venerable Archbishop Fulton Sheen once made this keen observation: "When a man loves a woman, it follows that the nobler the woman, the nobler the love; the higher the demands made by the woman, the more worthy a man must be. That is why woman is the measure of the level of our civilization."[22] This, of course, also applies to not only the women men want to marry but also Lady Mary. When men love the most noble of women, the bar of culture is raised to new heights.

Archbishop Sheen's insight also sheds light on something Pope Pius X said. "If we were to lose Mary," the pope explained, "the world would wholly decay. Virtue would disappear, especially holy purity and virginity, connubial love and fidelity. The mystical river through which God's graces

---

22   Fulton J. Sheen, *The World's First Love*, 2nd ed. (San Francisco: Ignatius Press, 2010), 184.

flow to us would dry up. The brightest star would disappear from heaven, and darkness would take its place."[23] Sadly, we need not look too far to see what a culture that has lost Mary looks like and why it is so essential that we bring her back into our hearts and homes.

---

23   Quoted in Mindszenty, *Face of the Heavenly Mother*, 83.

PART II

Mary's Geopolitical Influence

Chapter 4

Our Lady of Guadalupe

Islam and Evangelization

O ne of the most difficult things about studying Mary is that much of her story is old history. Among these ancient tales are intriguing patterns. There is usually a humble soul involved—a weathered farmer, a handful of children, or an uneducated young girl—who reports seeing a woman more beautiful than he or she had ever imagined. In cases of warfare, the battles have a turning point when the Christian underdogs, who have done their homework, see the tide of the battle turn due to some inexplicable event—perhaps a vision or a change in weather. And the messages have uniformity to them: pray for the conversion of sinners, pray the Rosary, build a church. Our Lady never asks to be worshiped but rather points to her Son and the love He poured out for us on the Cross. Despite these regular patterns, there are still wonderful layers of intrigue, connection, and coincidence that show up when one looks at the bigger picture.

Most Christians are familiar—even if just vaguely—with the stories of Guadalupe, Lourdes, and Fatima. What we are generally not familiar with are the deeper connections these events have with world history. Like peeling back the layers of an onion, the connections to Our Lady's work in and around these instances are nothing short of astounding. Each of these engages such thorny issues as Islamic expansion, massive conversion of the seemingly inconvertible, and the continued threat of Communism.

The Threat of Islam

One of the greatest threats to Christianity today is Islam. With the rise of the Islamic State of Iraq and Syria (ISIS), many martyrs have been made through vicious attacks. Entire Christian communities have been wiped out or displaced as their churches are ransacked, and ancient holy sites are desecrated or destroyed beyond recognition. The notion of jihad, a holy war against infidels, continues to develop before our very eyes as our smart phones relay these atrocities almost in real time.

A survey of Mary's relationship with Islam raises interesting questions. On the one hand, it is clear that she is something of a bridge between Christians and Muslims. There is a book dedicated to her in the Qur'an, and she is mentioned in Islam's holy book thirty-four times. In the Qur'an, Mary is held up as a model of holiness, second only to Mohammad's daughter, Fatima, while Mary's perpetual virginity is affirmed. As one Sunni scholar, Yusuf Ali, says of Mary, "Chastity was her special virtue: with a son of virgin birth, she and Jesus became a miracle in all nations."[1]

---

1   James L. Heft, "The Intellectual Life and Mary," *International Marian Research Institute*, October 16, 2009, https://www.udayton.edu/imri/mary/i/intellectual-life-and-mary.php.

On the other hand, there are clear indications that Mary has been a force in the Christian effort to hold back Islam's invading armies. History is pockmarked with battle after battle where Marian intercession has prevailed over Muslims. Among them is the Battle of Vienna, headed by Polish king Jan Sobieski, where the Poles prevented the Ottomans from moving deeper into Europe. There are also plenty of lesser-known battles, such as King Louis the Great of Hungary's rout of eighty thousand Turks by his meager army of twenty thousand, which led to the construction (or reconstruction, depending on which story you read) of the Mariazell Shrine, known as the Lourdes of Central Europe, in 1363.

Recently, much attention has been given to the 1571 Battle of Lepanto, where the outnumbered Christian alliance defeated the Muslim Turks, protecting Europe from Islam. This battle was certainly miraculous and should be a great sign of hope for us living in these uncertain times, but it is part of a much larger (and lesser-known) story that has a fascinating connection to Our Lady of Guadalupe.

The story starts in 711. Islamic forces made their way into Spain from Africa, conquering much of the Iberian Peninsula up into France. The Muslims, known generally as Moors or Saracens, reigned over most of Spain for more than five centuries while Christian crusaders had little to no traction in reclaiming their once Catholic land.

Devotion to Mary among the Christians started at first as a trickle but increased rapidly after the story spread of a battle at Tora, Spain, in 1003, where the Christians were outnumbered by the enemy (which included a large number of

Christian mercenaries fighting against their own). The story has come down to us by a monk named Andrew of Fleury, who wrote about the miraculous powers of St. Benedict, the patron of his abbey.[2]

As the decades wore on, more and more battles were won as Christian armies began to invoke Mary's name and image on the battlefield. Then around 1212, King Alfonso VIII took Mary as his patroness, fighting under a standard bearing her image. After centuries of very little to show for his efforts, King Alfonso and his Spanish army were finally victorious in taking back large areas of terrain. The Reconquista had begun!

Spain's Christians emphasized Our Lady's power in paintings, hymns, battle cries, military standards, and prayers. As they gained a foothold in the country, Spanish kings—starting with Ferdinand III (who was later proclaimed a saint) and then his son Alphonse X—made it clear that they weren't just followers of Mary but Marian kings under a Marian monarchy. They knew well who was behind their successes, and they honored her wherever they could, particularly in the form of churches. Whenever they were victorious, the mosques of the conquered cities were turned into churches and named for Our Lady.

Beyond the battlefields, story after story of the era tells of the Virgin freeing shackled prisoners and saving those who could see no escape from an imminent death at the hands of the Moors. One story even tells of a commander who,

---

2   Amy G. Remensnyder, *La Conquistadora* (London: Oxford University Press, 2014), 22.

late in the day, saw that the sun would set before the battle could be won. Kneeling down, he prayed that Our Lady would "stop the day" so he and his men could be victorious. As with Joshua against the Amorites, the sun was halted and the battle won.

"Christians all across Europe," Amy Remensnyder explains in her book *La Conquistadora*, "knew that the Virgin's maternal love shattered chains and defied prison walls, bringing solace and freedom to captives. Miracle after miracle demonstrates her compassionate presence in this traumatic arena of wartime experience."[3]

Finally, in 1492, under the military standard of Mary, Christianity retook Spain after 781 years of Islamic occupation. But before the Spaniards were victorious, something miraculous happened around 1326 in a newly liberated area of central Spain known as Extremadura. A shepherd had an apparition of the most beautiful woman in dazzling white. She told him that she wanted her image to be exhumed and a church built on the site. The humble shepherd told a priest, and he unearthed the strongbox containing the image of Our Lady along with a parchment detailing its provenance and illustrious history. So what was this image? According to legend, it was another miraculous image painted by St. Luke. (Our Lady of Częstochowa and the Vladimir Icon of the Mother of God are also attributed to St. Luke.) In the sixth century, Pope Gregory the Great gave it to the bishop of Seville, St. Leander. When the city was attacked by the Moors in 711, Christians hastily

3   Ibid., 100–101.

buried her out of harm's way up in the hills near the Guadalupe River.

After the image was exhumed and honored in a church,
more miracles abounded, including victory after victory
against the Moors. Finally, in January 1492, the last Saracen
holdout in Spain was conquered.

In June 1492, Ferdinand and Isabel made a pilgrimage to venerate the holy image in thanksgiving for their
victory in Granada. Later that year, King Ferdinand and
Queen Isabella understood that Our Lady was backing
their efforts and decided to finance an adventurous plan to
evangelize new worlds by funding Christopher Columbus.
It was that same year—as every schoolchild knows—that
"Columbus sailed the ocean blue." Despite how Columbus has been portrayed over the years, it's clear that his
Catholic faith and devotion to Our Lady was vital and
vigorous. Father John Hardon, in a presentation about
Columbus's Catholicity and deep devotion to the Blessed
Virgin Mary, said that every primary source about Columbus makes it clear that he felt strongly that he was chosen
especially by God to spread the gospel of Christ far and
wide to pagan lands.[4]

Columbus's faith was not a private affair. Admiral
Columbus would gather his crew every evening as the sun
set to sing the "Salve Regina" hymn to their Protectress.

---

4   John Hardon, "The Blessed Virgin Mary and the Catholic
      Discovery of America, Talk 4," *Real Presence Association*, 2003,
      http://www.therealpresence.org/archives/Christopher_Columbus/
      Christopher_Columbus_004.htm.

Two of the three ships were named for her, the *Santa María* and the *Niña* ("the girl"). And with the discovery of new land, Columbus would bestow on it a Catholic name, such as San Salvador, or Santa María de la Concepción. On a subsequent voyage, Columbus would call an archipelago east of Cuba "Our Lady's Sea," an unusually circular island Santa María Rotunda, and another island whose mountains resembled those around the Shrine of Our Lady of Guadalupe, *Guadipea*.[5] Sadly, Columbus's names for Watling's Island, Rum Cay, and elsewhere did not stick.

Upon return to Spain after his first voyage, despite the acclaim he was receiving for his feat, Columbus dutifully fulfilled a promise he had made to the Virgin when caught in a storm at sea. He promised that if he and his men were saved from disaster, he would make a pilgrimage to Our Lady of Guadalupe, and so he did.

Columbus was devoted to Mary until the end of his life and even included in his will plans for a church to Our Lady of the Immaculate Conception to be built on the island of Hispaniola. Sadly, his desires were never enacted.

Columbus was followed by another explorer, Hernán Cortés, and his entourage of ships and men. Here again, despite the Spaniard's transgressions against the natives—and many were egregious—the heart of his mission was to convert the natives of the newly found lands.

---

5   John M. Samaha, "Marian Devotion of Christopher Columbus," *International Marian Research Institute*, https://www.udayton. edu/imri/mary/c/christopher-columbus-marian-devotion-of.php.

Although the Spanish did not know what they might find among the natives, nothing prepared them for the sacrifices they encountered among the Aztecs. The gods of the Aztecs, it was said, demanded human blood. Even the sun god demanded blood in order for the sun to rise. Nearly one thousand people—mostly the poor, slaves, and children—were sacrificed *daily* to slake the bloodthirsty gods. Never has the conquest of a culture appeared nobler, particularly when the Spanish knew they had the one true God to offer these people—a God who, rather than exacting human sacrifice, offered His own body and blood for the sake of humanity.

After the violent struggle to conquer the Aztec people, in one short generation, the Aztec gods were dismantled, and the true God was being taught by Franciscan missionaries. Their efforts, however, were met with little traction, since the Aztecs saw the Spanish as invaders who caused them much suffering. As a result, the invaders' religion wasn't very attractive. Additionally, polygamy was rampant, and few natives saw any reason to change their ways. It was to this conquered culture that Our Lady of Guadalupe showed herself as a mother, bridging the gap between the Aztec and the Spanish people in her apparition to Juan Diego.

Juan Diego was a native who was considered something of a turncoat because he fully embraced the faith of the Spaniards. The divisions among the Spanish and the Aztecs were deep and seemingly insurmountable—that is, until Our Lady appeared to the humble widower on Tepeyac Hill. The hill itself had been the site of goddess worship among the

Aztecs. As ever, Mary was marking her claim—not as a god-dess, but as the Mother of God. As she greeted Juan Diego warmly in the early morning, she said,

> My dear little son, I love you. I desire you to know who I am. I am the ever-virgin Mary, Mother of the true God who gives life and maintains its existence. He created all things. He is in all places. He is Lord of Heaven and Earth. I desire a church in this place where your people may experience my compassion. All those who sincerely ask my help in their work and in their sorrows will know my Mother's Heart in this place. Here I will see their tears; I will console them and they will be at peace.[6]

Juan Diego reported Our Lady's request to the bishop, who asked for a sign to prove that what he was saying was true. "The bishop shall have his sign," Mary assured Juan Diego. "Go to the top of the hill," she told him when they next met, "and cut the flowers that are growing there. Bring them then to me." Of course, what happened next is no mystery. Mary arranged the Castilian roses (which had never been seen in Mexico before), and later, when Juan Diego opened his tilma before the bishop, the roses came tumbling out, revealing her image miraculously imprinted on the tilma.

When looking at the image of Our Lady of Guadalupe, the Spanish saw one set of symbols so familiar to most

---

6   "Our Lady of Guadalupe," *Catholic Online*, http://www.catholic .org/about/guadalupe.php.

Catholics that they are hardly noteworthy: a veiled woman, pregnant, head down and hands together in a prayerful posture—a typical sort of Marian image. But to the Aztecs, who were largely unfamiliar with Mary, an entirely different set of symbols spoke to them. Rather than books with an alphabet, the Aztecs wrote in symbols to tell stories. When they "read" the tilma, a whole story unfolded. First, they saw a woman with her head down, which meant that she was not a goddess but a mortal woman. Her long hair symbolized that she was virgin, but she also had a bow tied around her waist, showing that she was pregnant. And on her swollen stomach, a flower symbolized perfection and divinity. In this way, the Aztecs were able to "read" very quickly the story of this woman—that she was a pregnant virgin carrying God.

Additionally, the stars on Mary's blue mantle were not placed at random. The Aztec priestly class would have been able to see that they accorded with the time of the sky at the exact moment when Our Lady appeared to Juan Diego.

Juan Diego's uncle asked Our Lady her name as she healed him from a deadly disease. She told him her name was Santa María de Guadalupe ("St. Mary of Guadalupe"). Many believe that what Mary said was mistranslated by the Spanish. Instead of Guadalupe, they claim, she really said *Coatlallope*, meaning "one who steps on snakes." It doesn't seem too much of a stretch to suspect that Mary—who was keenly aware of the double entendre the name would carry for the Spanish and Aztecs, respectively—meant for the overlap to happen. After all, Mary placed symbols in her image on Juan Diego's tilma that spoke to the Aztecs, while others resonated with the Spaniards. Our Lady, through her image, inspired possibly the largest mass conversion in history: an estimated four to ten million souls came to the Catholic faith.

As for the meaning of the name *Guadalupe*, some have made the fascinating suggestion that it is actually Arabic for "hidden river." Such a name suits well an image hidden for six centuries that, once unearthed, unleashed a steady and powerful force of grace.

One of the signs that the conversions brought about by Our Lady of Guadalupe in Mexico had staying power and weren't just superficial is that polygamous family units were reordered into monogamous relationships. What the Aztecs had resisted fiercely when it was presented by the Franciscan missionaries was embraced after the revelation of Juan Diego's tilma.

Finally, to tie a bow in this historical thread, we return to the Battle of Lepanto in 1571. The Holy League, formed by Pope Pius V and Christian maritime states, engaged in a massive naval battle under the leadership of Don John (or Juan) of Austria against the Turks. Don John was the illegitimate brother of the Spanish king Philip II, who gave him the naval appointment. The night before the battle, the Holy League soldiers and Pius V diligently prayed the Rosary, knowing that they were significantly outnumbered. Despite their much smaller force, the Christians were victorious because they had more sophisticated guns and canons and better marksmanship. After the battle was won through Our Lady's intercession, Philip II, knowing his debt to the Virgin, offered to Our Lady of Guadalupe (in Spain) a lantern captured from the Turk's flagship. Certainly King Philip knew the power unleashed by the "hidden river," which had been the font of so much success. Pope Pius V instituted the feast of Our Lady of Victory to commemorate the event.

Of course, the Battle of Lepanto did not put an end to the Muslim menace. In 1683, the Polish king Jan Sobieski would go to battle again in Vienna against the Turks. His army, too, would prepare for battle with their rosaries in one hand and weapons in the other. Prior to the battle, Sobieski made a quick visit to pray to Our Lady of Częstochowa. After visiting the famous shrine to Mary, he gave word to his soldiers that they should enter into the battle with this prayer on their lips: "In the name of Mary, Lord God, help!"[7]

Yet again, despite being outnumbered, Sobieski and his army defeated the Turks on September 11 (a date that was made infamous when Islamic extremists attacked the West more than three hundred years later). King Sobieski and his Winged Hussars (swift soldiers on horseback) swooped in and broke the Ottoman lines, leaving huge numbers of dead and demoralizing the living. After weeks of siege, the battle for Vienna was over in a few short hours. The victory led to the Treaty of Karlowitz in 1699, giving the Hapsburgs Croatia, Slavonia, and parts of Hungary. After the battle, Sobieski wrote to Pope Innocent XI, saying that he fought for God's

---

7   Marian Załęcki, "Theology of a Marian Shrine, Częstochowa," *Marian Library Studies* 8 (1976): 35–311, http://ecommons.udayton .edu/cgi/viewcontent.cgi?article=1059&context=ml_studies.

cause and Mary's honor: "I came, I saw, but God and Mary conquered."[8]

The clash with the Muslim Turks heated up again in the early eighteenth century. In 1716, a new Turkish army of one hundred sixty thousand soldiers invaded Hapsburg territory. Prince Eugene of Savoy and ninety-one thousand Austrians, Hungarians, Serbians, and Croats set out to defend Christendom. After outflanking the Turks and encircling them inside a fortress, the Turks were annihilated. Only fifty thousand limped back to Constantinople.

Prince Eugene, who went to confession and prayed a Rosary before every battle, was just getting started. Because of his piety, a common saying developed among his men: "Prince Eugene is praying the rosary; there's going to be a battle."[9] In a sweeping three-month period of conquest, Prince Eugene liberated city after city in Hungary from centuries of Turkish control. All of Hungary was free from Turkish forces in the week of October 7–11, drawing a comparison to the Battle of Lepanto one hundred fifty years prior. In celebration, Pope Clement XI raised the feast of Our Lady of Victory to be celebrated by the universal Church under the name of Our Lady of the Holy Rosary.

Prince Eugene went on to more miraculous victories, including the triumph over Turkish forces in Belgrade in

---

8   "Institution of the Angelus," *Roman Catholic Saints*, http://www
     .roman-catholic-saints.com/institution-of-the-angelus.html.

9   Joseph Mindszenty, *The Face of the Heavenly Mother* (New York:
     Philosophical Library, 1951), 81.

1717, which ended Turkish rule in the Balkans, breaking their control over Europe.

New Battles With Islam

Unfortunately, the battles of old did not put a definitive end to clashes with Islam. They are as aggressive and deadly as they have ever been, so Mary's intercession is needed once again. Just a few years ago, Nigerian bishop Oliver Dashe Doeme told the international press about his own experience with the Rosary: "Towards the end of last year I was in my chapel before the Blessed Sacrament . . . praying the rosary, and then suddenly the Lord appeared." In the vision, Jesus didn't say anything at first but extended a sword toward Doeme, who in turn reached out for it. "As soon as I received the sword, it turned into a rosary," the bishop said, adding that Jesus then told him three times: "Boko Haram is gone."

"I didn't need any prophet to give me the explanation," Bishop Doeme said. "It was clear that with the rosary we would be able to expel Boko Haram." The group is responsible for kidnapping three hundred schoolgirls, some of whom have been returned either pregnant or with babies conceived by their captors, while still others remain missing and unaccounted for. Additionally, more than one hundred thousand of the Christians in Bishop Doeme's diocese have fled elsewhere for safety, leaving roughly sixty thousand to fend off the radical Islamic militants.

There are also new stories pouring out of Iraq as Islamic State–controlled territories are losing ground and Iraqis are reclaiming Christian territories. One miraculous story is of seven young college women who hid under beds for eight hours as Islamic State fighters used their room as a hideout during an assault on the city of Kirkuk on October 21, 2016. "When ISIS entered our room, they didn't see us, [and] we feel that the Virgin Mary closed their eyes from seeing us," one young woman recalled.[10] Father Roni Momika, who was in cell phone contact with two of the girls as they hid, said, "The Virgin Mary was with them."[11]

Clearly, not all Muslims are radical militants. Lebanese journalist Mahassen Haddara wrote a prayer to Jesus and His Mother in the wake of the martyrdom of Father Jacques Hamel in France in 2016:

> O Mary! Jesus! Do not delay!
>
> We beg you, Virgin Lady of the women of the world, ask Jesus to quickly come to us, because we are no longer able to endure what is going on . . . Our world, from Jerusalem to Iraq suffers from divisions . . .
> Our churches and mosques are desecrated, our priests are being killed, our children are being killed, and we are helpless . . .
>
> We beg you, Mother, help us with your prayer . . .

---

10   "Christian Girls Who Hid From ISIS: Blessed Mother Helped Us," *National Catholic Register*, October 24, 2016, http://www .ncregister.com/daily-news/christian-girls-who-hid-from -isis-blessed-mother-helped-us.

11   Ibid.

> Jesus, do not be late . . .
> Come to us, because we suffer.[12]

This prayer is a sign of hope that many conversions are ripe among Muslims. Islam in general has very little tenderness. The Muslim faith exacts submission, not love, not filial care, and certainly there is no mother to offer tenderness, hope, and healing in the face of harsh realities. Mary remains a bridge in mysterious ways.

---

12   "Muslim Journalist Publishes Her Prayer for Help, Made to Jesus and Mary," *Aleteia*, August 13, 2016, http://aleteia.org/ 2016/08/13/lebanese-journalist-publishes-her-prayer-for -help-made-to-jesus-and-mary.

CHAPTER 5

Our Lady of Lourdes

Humbling the Proud

On February 17, 1941, the Nazis arrested Father Maximilian Kolbe. The last piece of writing to come from his pen before he was sent to Auschwitz was "The Holy Spirit Is the Uncreated Immaculate Conception."[1] For decades, Father Kolbe had wrestled with the question of what it meant when Our Lady of Lourdes said to St. Bernadette, "I am the Immaculate Conception." After all, wouldn't it make more sense for her to say, "I was immaculately conceived?" And yet, it seems that with this final sentence, Father Kolbe finally found the answer to his lingering question just in the nick of time. Seven months later, Father Kolbe would be dead at Auschwitz after voluntarily taking the place of a father who was to be put to death via starvation at the camp.

Before getting to how this question was answered, we need to start from the beginning of the story. Like we saw in

---

1   H. M. Manteau-Bonamy, *Immaculate Conception and the Holy Spirit* (Libertyville, IL: Marytown Press, 2001), 3.

the last chapter, Mary doesn't waste opportunities; she plants seeds over the ages. Sometimes it can take centuries for these seeds to come to fruition.

The story of Lourdes starts centuries before young Bernadette encountered the beautiful woman at Massabielle. While the area of Massabielle was known as a decrepit place during Bernadette's time—fit only to feed swine and gather kindling—it hadn't always been regarded as such.

In 778, Charlemagne approached the Muslim stronghold in the Aquitaine region of Southern France. On the edge of the Pyrenees mountains, the fortress of Massabielle was the last refuge of the indefatigable Saracen fighters who had occupied the area for forty years. Led by the fierce Saracen Mirat, the fortress was impregnable. Mirat was determined to fight to the death because he had made an oath in the name of Mohammed that he would never surrender to a mortal man. Charlemagne and his soldiers were left with one option: starve them out.

After weeks passed, resources inside the fort were running low. An eagle dropped a trout inside to the desperate men. The starving Mirat, rather than devour the fish, flippantly threw it back at the enemy soldiers, as if to indicate that their food was still plenty in hopes that it would break their resolve, and Charlemagne and his men would leave. Suspecting a trick, the local bishop of Le Puy, Roracius, requested an audience with Mirat. After seeing the sorry state of the Saracens, but knowing of Mirat's oath, the bishop said, "Brave prince, you have sworn never to yield to any mortal man. Could you not with honor make your surrender to an immortal Lady? Mary, Queen of Heaven, has her throne at Le Puy, and I am her humble minister there."[2] Mirat saw that agreeing would free him from his oath; he promptly surrendered to the Queen of Heaven. He and his men became subjects to the Queen; all were baptized, and Mirat was given a new name, Lorus. Charlemagne knighted him, and Lorus went on to command the Fortress of Massabielle. It is the name Lorus from which the name Lourdes comes.

More than a thousand years would pass before the Queen of Heaven would perform the miraculous at the Fortress of Massabielle. It was there that the young Bernadette Soubirous had her visions of Our Lady of Lourdes—visions that have led innumerable souls back to their faith and health through the healing waters of the spring that miraculously appeared when Bernadette obediently scratched the earth during an apparition. While the precise meaning of the link back to the conversion of Mirat and his men might only become known to us in heaven, the connection between the two events hardly seems coincidental, given the current state of our world and the resurgence of radical Islam. It is not the only time that Our Lady has appeared in a place that featured the conversion of a well-known Muslim to Catholicism; we will see another in the next chapter.

Among the fifteen Vatican-approved apparitions of Our Lady, four occurred in France. Another in Italy was directly related to one of the French apparitions. These five happened

---

2 "Lourdes: The Islamic Connection," *Christian Order* (blog), February 2005, http://www.christianorder.com/features/features_2005/features_feb05_bonus.html.

within a thirty-five-year time span. So what was happening in France to spark such heavenly intervention?

During the French Revolution and the Reign of Terror at the end of the eighteenth century, thousands of martyrs spilled their blood for their Catholic faith. The revolution's violent antimonarchy frenzy spread beyond France's borders, creating tumult across Europe. France continued to convulse for nearly a century, with barricades thrown up in the streets at the slightest provocation, violence and bloodshed starting all over again. Napoleon also brought with him great strife, and fresh riots sparked by the Communists who organized the Paris Commune of 1871 left the city reeling. Through all this, the Church was in turmoil, with anti-Catholic and anticlerical laws strictly enacted. The state usurped control over much of the Church's property, including thousands of Catholic schools and monasteries. The extensive influence the Church once had in France vanished because it no longer had the schools and other social institutes that had flourished for centuries. Many people lost their faith. The few French Catholics who remained looked to Rome for succor and assurance in the face of open persecution.

Rue du Bac, Paris, France (1830)

The first of these French apparitions occurred when Mary visited Sister Catherine Labouré, a humble Vincentian nun, in 1830. Mary told Catherine that the next forty years would be a time of great tumult and sadness in the world, but not to be afraid because even when things were at their darkest, Mary would be with her. Mary also gave her an image that she wanted made into a medal to be shared with the faithful.

It would come to be known as the Miraculous Medal. Initially, twenty-two thousand pieces were made. Within the first year, that number swelled to more than two million. No one knows how many Miraculous Medals have been cast today. Sister Catherine was later canonized for her heroic virtue, as she ardently lived a humble life serving the elderly. Members of her community, save her spiritual director, were largely unaware that it was to her that Our Lady appeared (although they knew the famous medal had come from one of their own). After Sister Catherine's death, many of the nuns greatly regretted that they had not treated her well, also attesting to Sister Catherine's humility and heroic virtue.

St. Andrew of the Woods, Rome, Italy (1842)

The next apparition took place in 1842 and was directly related to the first. Alphonse Tobie Ratisbonne was a twenty-eight-year-old Jewish man in the prime of his life who had just gotten engaged to marry. He was a lawyer from a wealthy family and was charming, good looking, and good humored. Prior to his wedding, he decided to spend the winter in Malta. At all costs, however, he wanted to avoid Rome because he hated Catholicism; the conversion and ordination of his brother Theodore had only fanned the flames of his already intense hatred of the Faith. But somehow, because of a delay with boats out of Naples and his own restlessness, Ratisbonne found himself in the Eternal City. With a few days to spend before his boat left for Malta, Ratisbonne caught up with some friends, including Baron Theodore de Bussières, who gave Ratisbonne a Miraculous Medal as a challenge to Ratisbonne's fierce anti-Catholicism. The baron argued, "If it is just superstition, then it won't harm you in the least to wear this or to read the *memorare* prayer." Then on January 20, 1842, while waiting for the baron in the church of Sant'Andrea delle Fratte ("St. Andrew of the Woods"), Ratisbonne saw a vision of the Blessed Virgin. The brief vision of blinding beauty didn't include an exchange of words, but by the end of it, Ratisbonne said he knew "all the secrets of divine pity."[3] He immediately converted to Catholicism, joined the priesthood, and moved to Israel with a ministry to convert the Jews. Ratisbonne's conversion was so significant that even the pope heard of it and wanted to learn more about this "miraculous medal" and the nun who had it cast. The medal's popularity swelled and Sister Catherine's waned as she remained just another cloistered nun among many.

La Salette, France (1846)

The next apparition at La Salette happened four years later, in 1846. High up in the French Alps, Mary appeared to two children—Maximin, eleven; and Mélanie, fourteen—as they tended sheep. What they saw when they came upon her was unique among apparitions; she sat as a lady sobbing, her hands covering her face in grief. Indeed, looking at the turmoil in France and beyond, Mary had much to grieve over. France's anti-Catholic streak had even reached the small village of La Salette, where Mass and the sacraments were

---

3   Joseph Dirvin, *Saint Catherine Labouré of the Miraculous Medal* (Charlotte, NC: TAN Books, 1984), http://www.ewtn.com/library/MARY/CATLABOU.HTM.

neglected as fewer and fewer people valued the faith of their fathers. Cursing was preferred to prayer, sexual license erased purity, and greed and self-indulgence superseded piety and sacrifice. Even the children to whom Mary appeared had little faith or formation. They rarely went to Mass and were barely able to muddle through the Our Father or Hail Mary. The messages from La Salette are significant because of their length and detail. In them, Mary warned the children that if the people continued to dishonor her Son—namely, by disregarding the Sabbath and swearing with the Lord's name (sins that in our current climate of moral decadence seem so innocent today)—famine and disease would cover the land. Mary said, "Come to me, my children. Do not be afraid. I am here to tell something of the greatest importance. If my people will not obey, I shall be compelled to loose my Son's arm."[4] She continued,

> If the harvest is spoiled, it is your own fault. I warned you last year by means of the potatoes. You paid no heed. Quite the reverse, when you discovered that the potatoes had rotted, you swore, you abused my Son's name. They will continue to rot, and by Christmas this year there will be none left.
>
> If you have grain, it will do no good to sow it, for what you sow the beasts will devour, and any part of it that springs up will crumble into dust when you thresh it.

4   "What Is the Story of Our Lady of La Salette?," *Catholic Straight Answers*, http://catholicstraightanswers.com/what-is-the-story -of-our-lady-of-la-salette.

A great famine is coming. But before that happens,
the children under seven years of age will be seized
with trembling and die in their parent's arms. The
grownups will pay for their sins by hunger. The grapes
will rot, and the walnuts will turn bad.[5]

Then Our Lady added, "If people are converted, the rocks
will become piles of wheat, and it will be found that the
potatoes have sown themselves."[6] After a further exchange,
including instruction for the children's prayers, Mary walked
away up a steep path before disappearing into a bright light.

The children dutifully shared their important message,
which was spread far and wide. The rock where Our Lady
was sitting later revealed a spring that had not been there
before. From the spring's water came miraculous healings.
Among the many miracles was the transformation of the
people, who returned to their faith. One of the reasons
this apparition soared in popularity was because the pre-
dictions made by Our Lady came true. The potato famine
did happen—particularly in Ireland and France from 1845
to 1852—and cholera wracked Europe, killing hundreds of
thousands there and beyond, especially children.

Lourdes, France (1858)

The Immaculate Conception was a debated topic for centuries. Some scholars argued for it strenuously, while others
suggested that Mary was already honored enough, so making

---

5   Ibid.
6   Ibid.

it dogma would be superfluous. Even before the dogma was announced in 1854 by Pope Pius IX, many countries selected Our Lady of the Immaculate Conception as their patroness, including the United States on May 13, 1846. Apparently, however, Mary thought the dogma was important enough to confirm it just a few years after Pius pronounced it by visiting a fourteen-year-old uneducated peasant girl, Bernadette Soubirous. Mary appeared to her in a series of eighteen apparitions, and in the last, she gave Bernadette her name: "I am the Immaculate Conception."

In one of Mary's apparitions to Bernadette, Our Lady asked her to dig in the dirt. As she dug, a spring trickled through the dirt. The water from the spring proved itself to be miraculous, healing those who bathed in it. Even today, six million visitors come to Lourdes annually. The humble Bernadette and the healing waters of Lourdes confounded both the medical community and the enlightened philosophes, such as Émile Zola, who had poisoned the minds of millions with atheism and an uncritical worship of science. Zola even made a visit to Lourdes in the hopes of discrediting it, only to witness the miraculous healing of a woman suffering from three incurable diseases. Upon seeing her restored to wellness, he puffed, "To me she is still ugly," and dismissed the miraculous event. He dug his heels in even deeper, saying, "Were I to see all the sick at Lourdes cured, I would not believe in a miracle."[7]

---

7   George Sim Johnston, "Belief and Unbelief I: Émile Zola at Lourdes," *Crisis Magazine*, December 1, 1989, http://www.crisis magazine.com/1989/belief-and-unbelief-i-emile-zola-at-lourdes.

Pontmain, France (1871)

Intriguingly, the title for this apparition is Our Lady of Hope. This was near the end of France's most tumultuous period—the forty years that St. Catherine Labouré had been warned about. Mary appeared in the night sky above the town of Pontmain in the north of France, near the front of the advancing Franco-Prussian War (War of 1870). Rumor had it that the Prussians intended to strike the area the next day. It was the darkest hour of the war, with many French soldiers deserting their posts in anticipation of the Prussians' attack. Already Paris had been defeated, and two-thirds of the country was controlled by Prussia.

As night fell, the Barbedette family was taking care of their livestock when the elder son, Eugene, looked out the door of the barn and saw a beautiful woman smiling at him in the star-studded sky. Her gown was covered in stars, and she held out her hands like the image of Mary in the Miraculous Medal. Others came to see, but only four children were able to see the beautiful lady. The apparition lasted for three hours. In it, Mary didn't say a single word but held up a banner that stated, "But pray, my children. God will soon answer you. My Son allows Himself to be touched." That same night, Prussian forces ended their advance toward the Pontmain area at about the same time the apparition started. General Schmidt is reported to have said the next morning, "We cannot go farther. Yonder, in the direction of Brittany, there is an invisible 'Madonna' barring the way."[8] Of course, this begs the question, if she was invisible, how did they know she was there?

---

8   "Our Lady of Pontmain," *Wikipedia*, last modified January 18, 2016, https://en.wikipedia.org/wiki/Our_Lady_of_Pontmain.

Regardless, this Madonna brought an end to the battle and the war, and an armistice was signed five days later. As for the four children, two became priests, one became a nun, and the fourth became a housekeeper for one of the priests.

The apparition in Pontmain marked the end of the massive cultural and military upheaval in France. While more conflicts were to follow, a period of relative calm set in after a century of chaos and blood.

Meanwhile, as Mary was reassuring the faithful in France of her constant aid and warning those who would betray and neglect her Son, she was also setting the stage for a new priest to become her spiritual warrior twenty years later in the distant land of Poland.

St. Maximilian Kolbe

Maximilian Kolbe was born in 1894 in Poland. His life was marked by tremendous devotion to Our Lady. And even though he only went to Lourdes once, his life was mysteriously connected to the apparition site. Father G. M. Domanski, one of the directors of Kolbe's Militia Immaculata, said of him, "In 1914 his right thumb, which the doctors wanted to amputate, had been miraculously healed by an application of Lourdes water, thus making it possible for him to continue on to the priesthood. The ideal to which he devoted his entire life was based upon Mary's revelation of herself in her apparitions to Bernadette, to Sister Catherine Labouré, and to Alphonse Ratisbonne in Rome."[9]

---

9   H. M. Manteau-Bonamy, *Immaculate Conception and the Holy Spirit: The Marian Teachings of St. Maximilian Kolbe*, 3rd ed. (Libertyville, IL: Marytown Press, 2008), 10.

While many have viewed St. Kolbe as going too far and giving Our Lady credit for things reserved for Christ, his work has been vindicated by the Marian encyclicals, writings, and declarations made by the Holy See that came shortly after his martyrdom. Pope Paul VI went so far as to call St. Maximilian "clairvoyant" for his rich articulation of Mary that would be confirmed by the Second Vatican Council, while Pope John Paul II later called him an "apostle of a new Marian era." Mariologist J. Lazure, capturing the sentiment of the time and the thoughts of many churchmen in 1954, said, "The Immaculate Conception implies in Mary the existence of inexhaustible riches which we have not even guessed at up to now."[10] Much of this, however, was because of the work of St. Maximilian Kolbe.

So just what did the then Father Maximilian Kolbe say about Our Lady and the Immaculate Conception? While the answer to this question will be discussed in greater detail in chapter 9, the short answer is that he was determined to understand exactly what it meant for Our Lady to say to St. Bernadette, "I am the Immaculate Conception." For years, he searched and prayed for the answer. Initially, it became clear to him that the Immaculate Conception was not a superficial aspect of Mary (like the difference between brown or green eyes; no matter the color, the eye still serves to see). Rather, it was something essential to who she was, and if it were taken away, she would not be Mary.

Ultimately, through his final reflections before his death, he was able to come to the understanding that Mary, as the spouse

---

10   Ibid., viii–ix.

of the Holy Spirit, is so united to the third person of the Trinity that she is the Immaculate Conception by the direct work of the uncreated Immaculate Conception, the Holy Spirit Himself. The Holy Spirit is the original Immaculate Conception because He proceeds out of the love of Father and Son. In Kolbe's last words, he finally came upon the idea that the Holy Spirit was the *uncreated* Immaculate Conception, while His spouse, Mary, was the *created* Immaculate Conception. This understanding of the relationship between Mary and the Holy Spirit had strong implications for who Mary is, for, as the Polish saint explained, from the moment of her conception, Mary was fruitful through the Holy Spirit while simultaneously acting as a mirror to humanity of what the Holy Spirit looks like. Mary makes concrete and material that which is only spiritual in the person of the Holy Spirit.

In many ways, this argument echoed what St. Louis de Montfort had said about Mary centuries before: the Holy Spirit chose Mary "to be the dispenser of all He possesses, in such wise that she distributes to whom she wills, as much as she wills, as she wills and when she wills, all His graces and gifts."[11] Because of this special relationship, St. Maximilian went so far as to say that Mary is our one gate: "Our dependence upon Mary is greater than we can imagine. We receive all graces, absolutely all of them, from God through the Immaculate, who is our universal mediatrix with Jesus."[12]

---

11 Louis de Montfort, *True Devotion to Mary* (Charlotte, NC: TAN Books, 2010), 11.

12 Maximilian Kolbe, *Let Yourself Be Led by the Immaculate* (Kansas City: Angelus Press, 2013), Kindle ed., loc. 11.

Hints of St. Maximilian's ideas were seen in Pope Pius IX's dogmatic declaration of the Immaculate Conception when he wrote in 1854 that Mary is *"singularly* holy and most pure in soul and body . . . the only one who has become the dwelling place of *all* the graces of the most Holy Spirit."[13] As St. Maximilian explained further, when we say we go "to Jesus through Mary," it is the equivalent of saying we go "to Jesus through the Holy Spirit." Why? Because, as Dwight P. Campbell states, "the Holy Spirit acts only in and through his beloved spouse, with whom he is so closely united by reason of Mary's Immaculate Conception."[14]

Rather than shy away from the rich theology articulated by St. Maximilian Kolbe, the Second Vatican Council affirmed it, and Pope Paul VI emphasized it in *Marialis Cultus*:

> Examining more deeply still the mystery of the Incarnation, they saw in the mysterious relationship between the Spirit and Mary an aspect redolent of marriage, poetically portrayed by Prudentius: "The unwed Virgin espoused the Spirit," and they called her the "Temple of the Holy Spirit," an expression that emphasizes the sacred character of the Virgin, now the permanent dwelling of the Spirit of God. Delving deeply into the doctrine of the Paraclete, they saw that

---

13 Pope Pius IX, *Ineffabilis Deus*, December 8, 1854, after "Of a Supereminent Sanctity," http://www.ewtn.com/LIBRARY/ PAPALDOC/P9INEFF.htm (my italics).

14 Dwight P. Campbell, "The Holy Spirit and Mary," *Homiletic & Pastoral Review* (May 1993): 12–23, https://www.catholicculture .org/culture/library/view.cfm?recnum=4270.

from Him as from a spring there flowed forth the fullness of grace (cf. Lk. 1:28) and the abundance of gifts
that adorned her. Thus they attributed to the Spirit
the faith, hope and charity that animated the Virgin's
heart, the strength that sustained her acceptance of the
will of God, and the vigor that upheld her in her suffering at the foot of the cross.[15]

Pope Paul VI, knowing that there was much more work
to do on this subject, requested of the faithful—especially
pastors and theologians—to look deeper into Mariology: "It
is the task of specialists to verify and weigh the truth of this
assertion, but it is our task to exhort everyone, especially
those in the pastoral ministry and also theologians, to meditate more deeply on the working of the Holy Spirit in the
history of salvation, and to ensure that Christian spiritual
writings give due prominence to His life-giving action. Such
a study will bring out in particular the hidden relationship
between the Spirit of God and the Virgin of Nazareth, and
show the influence they exert on the Church."[16] The Holy
Father added that "from a more profound meditation on the
truths of the Faith will flow a more vital piety."[17]

Throughout the years, Mary has provided clues and insights
into who she is through these five apparitions and the prayerful intellectual work of popes and saints. They are hard to see
in isolation, but grouping these together only confirms the

---

15   Pope Paul VI, *Marialis Cultus*, February 2, 1974, #26, *EWTN*,
        https://www.ewtn.com/library/PAPALDOC/P6MARIAL.HTM.
16   Ibid., #27.
17   Ibid.

importance of understanding Mary as the Immaculate Conception and the spouse of the Holy Spirit.

It's clear that more work needs to be done not only in Mariology but also in areas of catechesis and making the culmination of the work that flowed from the French apparitions known—particularly St. Maximilian Kolbe's rich writings. One of the curiosities about the French apparitions is that two of them produced springs from which healing waters flow. While this phenomenon is not exclusive to Lourdes or La Salette, it is a telling symbol of the graces available to us through Our Lady, the Immaculate Conception.

CHAPTER 6

Our Lady of Fatima

Conquering Communism

A s we saw in the previous chapter, Lourdes was the site of the conversion of the Islamic commander Mirat. Fatima, too, was a place of Islamic conversion—this time of a Muslim princess who was won over to the Faith. The princess Fatima was captured by Christian forces when the Moors occupied Portugal. She was then betrothed to the Count of Ourem (the region in which the village of Fatima is located) and converted to Catholicism before their wedding in 1158. She took the baptismal name Oureana. Writer Christopher Ferrara offers one explanation as to why the Virgin Mother has appeared in these places of conversion. Mary came to Fatima, Ferrara says, not for the sake of ecumenism but for "the triumph of Christendom over the Muslim occupiers of Portugal."[1] Through this triumph, Our Lady of Fatima is proclaiming the importance of the conversion

---

1   "Lourdes: The Islamic Connection," *Christian Order*, February 2005, http://www.christianorder.com/features/features_2005/features_feb05_bonus.html.

of non-Catholics to the Faith. In the case of Fatima, however, the emphasis is not on Islam (as it was partially with Our Lady of Guadalupe) but on the Russian people.

There can be no doubt that the apparitions of Our Lady of Fatima to the three children—Jacinta, Francisco, and Lúcia—singled out the Communist Russians and their potential to spread many evils to the whole world. To further understand this story, however, we must go back to another miraculous image: Our Lady of Kazan.

Our Lady of Kazan

The image of Our Lady of Kazan was, like many miraculous images, extremely important to the Russian people. She was known to stop wars, famines, and disease. She originally came to Russia from Constantinople in the thirteenth century and was later lost when the Tartars came rolling through the steppe of Russia, raping and pillaging their way across the country.

Then in 1579, when the city of Kazan was destroyed by fire, a ten-year-old girl named Matrona had a dream of Our Lady of Kazan. In the dream, Mary told her where to find the image. After the first dream, the little girl told the local archbishop, who scoffed at the child's suggestion. Matrona had two more dreams about the image's location, prompting her and her mother to dig up the image themselves. It was buried in the ashes of the house that had protected it since the Tartar's arrival. Despite the passing years, the fire, and the ashes, the icon appeared like new.

The archbishop, upon seeing the dazzling image, repented for not believing the little girl and took it to the Church of St. Nicholas, where a blind man was cured the same day. Hermogen—the name of the priest at the Church of St. Nicholas—was later made the Metropolitan of Kazan and brought the image with him to the cathedral. The czar asked him to write down the details of the icon, which come down to us today.

Later, Hermogen and the icon moved to Moscow when he became the patriarch of the city and all of Russia. In invasion after invasion, Our Lady of Kazan protected the Russian people when she was venerated. In 1812, to commemorate another victory—this one against the Swedes—the icon was moved to Kazan Cathedral in St. Petersburg.

Eventually, it became clear that there were two icons of Our Lady of Kazan, both of exquisite value and beauty. Around 1904, one of the icons was lost. Some speculated that it was stolen for its jewels and burned. Then in 1917, the other icon went missing during the October Revolution as the Bolsheviks took hold of the country. It seems that whoever removed her did so wisely, because the Bolsheviks, in their effort to prove that God did not exist, burned the basilica that had been home to the icon (or one of the icons). One present at the fire reported, "As great sledges and rams knocked down the church, loudspeakers blared: 'You see, there is no God! We destroy the church of the so-called protectress of Russia, and nothing happens!'"[2] Interestingly, one of the copies of the icon showed up during World War II in the 1940s when the Nazis besieged the city; the Virgin of Kazan led a procession around Leningrad to pray for protection yet again.

---

2   "Our Lady of Kazan," *Orthodox Wiki*, last modified November 22, 2011, https://orthodoxwiki.org/Our_Lady_of_Kazan.

Disappearing icons, however, were viewed by the Orthodox Church and the peasantry as an omen of tragedies to
come. They were not mistaken in their judgment.[3]

What happened in Russia in the early 1900s was the perfect storm of civilizational crisis. A power vacuum was created
by the weak czar, Nicholas II, who was heavily influenced by
his wife, Alexandra; meanwhile, the czarina was influenced
by the enigmatic and evil Grigori Rasputin. Although there
were many warnings about Rasputin's character, the czarina
would not be dissuaded from his counsel because he had
helped bring some semblance of peace to her ailing son, the
heir. Bishop after bishop warned her about his duplicity and
his cunning nature, and bishop after bishop was demoted
and/or moved elsewhere. Rasputin's influence came to an
end when the czar's allies, tired of the demonic influence
he had upon the royal family, murdered him. Even in death,
Rasputin showed superhuman strength as he was poisoned
with arsenic, shot repeatedly, beaten about the head, and then
finally submerged in an icy river. His autopsy revealed water
in his lungs, showing that he had survived the earlier attempts
to kill him and died from drowning.

Eventually the czar was discredited and dethroned, and
his entire family was murdered by the Bolsheviks. In the
midst of this fog of war, a new military leader made his way
from Berlin via Finland to Russia. His name was Vladimir

---

3   There is another miraculous image of Our Lady in Russia, the Vlad-
     imir Icon of the Mother of God. It is also said to have been painted
     by St. Luke and has many miracles associated with it. It was not lost
     during the Bolshevik Revolution, but today is housed in Tretyakov
     Gallery, Moscow, in a former church on the museum grounds.

Ilyich Ulyanov, otherwise known as Lenin. In the wake of the czar's weakness came the Communist Bolsheviks, who used a combination of ruthlessness, Marxist philosophy, and clever propaganda to win the massive country to their deadly ideology.

Our Lady of Fatima

At the height of World War I, hundreds of thousands of men were mowed down when their outmoded military formations encountered the teeth of modern armaments. Military leaders, steeped in tradition and rigid formations, showed themselves unwilling to change their tactics. The result was a stalemate consisting of long battles and high casualties, with no end to the war in sight.

In May 1917, weary from the war tearing Europe apart, Pope Benedict XV finally made a special appeal to Our Lady:

> To Mary, who is the Mother of Mercy and omnipotent by grace, let loving and devout appeal go up from every corner of the earth—from noble temples and tiniest chapels, from royal palaces and mansions of the rich as from the poorest hut—from every place wherein a faithful soul finds shelter—from blood-drenched plains and seas. Let it bear to her the anguished cry of mothers and wives, the wailing of innocent little ones, the sighs of every generous heart: that her most tender and benign solicitude may be moved and the peace we ask for be obtained for our agitated world.[4]

---

4   Warren H. Carroll, *1917 Red Banners, White Mantle* (Front Royal, VA: Christendom Publications, 1981), 72.

Then on May 13, 1917, eight days later, "she came herself, in person."[5] Three children—Lúcia de Santos (nine) and her cousins, Francisco (seven) and Jacinta Marto (eight)—were tending sheep in a field when they saw a ball of fire near an oak tree. When they got closer, they saw it was a beautiful lady from heaven who asked them to come there again on the thirteenth of every month for the next six months. Identifying herself as "Our Lady of the Rosary," she urged the children to pray the Rosary, to do penance for the conversion of sinners, to have a church built, and to have Russia consecrated to her Immaculate Heart.

Our Lady said to the three children,

> I come to ask the consecration of Russia to my Immaculate Heart and the Communion of reparation on the first Saturdays. If they listen to my requests, Russia will be converted and there will be peace. If not she will scatter her errors through the world, provoking wars and persecutions of the Church. The good will be martyrized, the Holy Father will have much to suffer, various nations will be annihilated. In the end my Immaculate Heart will triumph. The Holy Father will consecrate Russia to me, and it will be converted, and a certain period of peace will be granted to the world.[6]

In another exchange with the children, the Blessed Mother asked them, "Do you wish to offer yourselves to God, to

---

5   Ibid.
6   Ibid., 82.

endure all the suffering that He may please to send you, as an act of reparation for the sins by which He is offended, and to ask for the conversion of sinners?"

"Yes, we do," they replied.

She explained further, "Then you will have much to suffer. But the grace of God will be your comfort. Say the Rosary every day, to obtain peace for the world, and the end of the war."[7]

Fatima's Secret

In addition to the initial requests, Our Lady also told the children what has since been called the Secret of Fatima. It is one secret made up of three parts. These parts ignited a firestorm of speculation and conspiracy theories that continue even today. The three-part secret was given by Lúcia to the Holy See for safe keeping, although all three aspects have since been revealed.

The first part of the secret was a vision of hell the children were allowed to experience. Although it lasted only an instant, Lúcia recounted that they were only able to endure it by remembering that Our Lady had also promised to show them heaven. Explaining hell, Lúcia wrote, "Plunged in this fire were demons and souls in human form, like transparent burning embers, all blackened or burnished bronze, floating about in the conflagration, now raised into the air by the flames that issued from within themselves together with great clouds of smoke, now falling back on every side like sparks in a huge fire, without weight or equilibrium, and

---

7   Ibid., 73.

amid shrieks and groans of pain and despair, which horrified us and made us tremble with fear."[8]

The second part of the secret related to the war that was to follow the First World War if people did not heed Our Lady's call for penance and prayer: "If people do not cease offending God, a worse one [war] will break out during the Pontificate of Pius XI. When you see a night illumined by an unknown light, know that this is the great sign given you by God that he is about to punish the world for its crimes, by means of war, famine, and persecutions of the Church and of the Holy Father."[9]

This secret went on to mention Russia and the lies and destruction the country's leaders would spread to the world if the country was not consecrated to Mary and the faithful did not make reparation for sin: "If my requests are heeded, Russia will be converted, and there will be peace; if not, she will spread her errors throughout the world, causing wars and persecutions of the Church. The good will be martyred; the Holy Father will have much to suffer; various nations will be annihilated. In the end, my Immaculate Heart will triumph. The Holy Father will consecrate Russia to me, and she shall be converted, and a period of peace will be granted to the world."[10]

---

8   For the full text of the three parts of the secret, see "Congrega-
     tion for the Doctrine of the Faith: The Message of Fatima,"
     The Holy See, May 13, 2000, http://www.vatican.va/roman
     _curia/congregations/cfaith/documents/rc_con_cfaith_doc
     _20000626_message-fatima_en.html.
9   Ibid.
10   Ibid.

The third part of the secret was related to the suffering and martyrdom of a "Bishop dressed in White," as well as the martyrdom of priests, religious, and laity:

> [We saw a] Bishop dressed in White "we had the impression that it was the Holy Father." Other Bishops, Priests, men and women Religious going up a steep mountain, at the top of which there was a big Cross of rough-hewn trunks as of a cork-tree with the bark; before reaching there the Holy Father passed through a big city half in ruins and half trembling with halting step, afflicted with pain and sorrow, he prayed for the souls of the corpses he met on his way; having reached the top of the mountain, on his knees at the foot of the big Cross he was killed by a group of soldiers who fired bullets and arrows at him, and in the same way there died one after another the other Bishops, Priests, men and women Religious, and various lay people of different ranks and positions. Beneath the two arms of the Cross there were two Angels each with a crystal aspersorium in his hand, in which they gathered up the blood of the Martyrs and with it sprinkled the souls that were making their way to God.[11]

These secrets were revealed in full in 2000.

The Miracle of the Sun

The culminating moment of the Fatima apparitions occurred on October 13, 1917. Seventy thousand pilgrims made their way to the site to see the miracle Our Lady had promised,

---

11   Ibid.

including many naysayers. The day started with a downpour, but then the miraculous happened. The clouds parted and the sun danced, shooting out rays of light, and then it appeared to be hurtling toward the earth. Everyone was terrified until the diving sun stopped just short of harming anyone. As the pilgrims looked around, the once-soaked ground was instantly dry. Photographs and testimonies of the event appeared in the national papers. Any doubts that pilgrims might have harbored about the truthfulness of the children and the authenticity of the apparition dried up when the sun came out.

Eventually, the war ended as Our Lady said it would, but no more than a month after the end of the Fatima apparitions, the Bolshevik Revolution took place in Russia, turning the country upside down. Millions were sent to "reeducation camps" known as gulags in Siberia, never to return (millions more died in the gulags than were killed by Hitler). Anything outside the bounds of atheistic materialism and brute force vanished from the country. Faith was banned, as Marx had explained, because it was "the opiate of the people." And just as Our Lady predicted, the Russians spread their lies to other countries, gobbling up satellite countries after World War II and adding on to the Soviet Union, trapping millions behind the Iron Curtain. There would be other countries split in two over Communism, such as Korea and Vietnam. Brazil, along with other Latin American countries, was threatened by "the Red Scare," but miraculously, Brazil escaped, while the likes of Cuba and Nicaragua became Communist.[12]

---

12   Clarence Hall, "Brazil: The Country that Saved Itself," *Reader's Digest*, 1964.

As usual, Our Lady had planted seeds and was just waiting for them to mature long before her apparitions at Fatima. The seed started with Our Lady of Częstochowa, also known as the Black Madonna. It was another Marian image that knew well the battle with Catholicism's enemies. For centuries, reports of miraculous events and healings had been associated with this image of Our Lady. Centuries of votive candles in front of the image have covered the original colors of the portrait with soot, giving Mary's fair complexion a dark hue.

The icon's history is as tumultuous as Poland's history, and the two are tightly intertwined. Although there are various versions of the story of what happened to this famous portrait, legend holds that the icon was originally painted by St. Luke on a tabletop that Jesus constructed. While Luke painted the Blessed Mother, the Virgin Mary told the Gospel writer everything about her life.

After centuries of obscurity, in 326, the painting was discovered by St. Helen when she went to Jerusalem to search for the true Cross of Christ. St. Helen then passed it down to her son Constantine, who later had it displayed on a wall in Constantinople while the city was under siege by the Barbarians. The invaders were quickly routed, and the image was given credit for saving the city. The image changed hands until Charlemagne is said to have gained possession of it, before passing it on to Prince Leo of Ruthenia (then Hungary).

In the eleventh century, Ruthenia was invaded, and the king, his small army, and the country were spared after praying to Our Lady for divine assistance. The invaders were covered in a cloud of darkness and, in their confusion, started to attack each other.

In the fourteenth century, Prince Władysław, Duke of Opole, prompted by a dream, requested that sixteen Pauline monks from Hungary bring the holy image to Poland while establishing the Jasna Góra (meaning "mountain of light") Monastery in 1382.

In 1430, Hussites attacked the monastery and tried to take the sacred portrait. One marauder struck the painting twice with a sword and was immediately and inexplicably struck dead. Those cuts and another arrow wound to the image are still visible today.

In 1655, Poland was overrun by Swedish marauders in the war that is known today as "The Deluge." The entire country, except for Jasna Góra, had been conquered by the Swedes. The monks miraculously held off the enemy forces for forty days, thereby changing the momentum of what had been a devastating war. Miraculously, the rest of Poland was then able to drive out the Swedes. This remarkable event prompted the coronation of Our Lady of Częstochowa, naming her the Queen of Poland in 1717, when the entire country was placed under her protection.

In 1920, as the Bolshevik army was approaching the Vistula River in Warsaw, an image of Our Lady of Częstochowa was seen in the clouds over the river on September 15, the Feast of Our Lady of Sorrows. After a series of battles, the Red Army was defeated in what is known today as the "Miracle at the Vistula."

During World War II, the Nazis prohibited pilgrims from going to Jasna Góra, although many still risked death by doing so. In 1945, after the liberation of Poland, 500,000 Poles went to the holy site in gratitude, followed by 1.5 million Poles who gathered a year later on September 8, 1946, to rededicate their country to the Immaculate Heart of Mary.

Under Soviet Communism in Poland, Communist leaders also tried to keep pilgrims from the site. Undaunted, the archbishop Karol Wojtyła (the future Pope St. John Paul II) and other Church leaders helped arrange a tour of the Black Madonna around Poland. Archbishop Wojtyła was intensely devoted to the Virgin Mary and her icon at Częstochowa.

It was this background that provided Wojtyła, as a Pole and as a man, with a strong Marian devotion (especially to Our Lady of Częstochowa) that changed the world. Wojtyła was intensely loyal to his country and deeply distrustful of the Soviets, having lived under the jackboot of Communism for many decades. He was intimately familiar with the Soviet machine and its ways of manipulating reality. For this reason, among others, the Soviets where scared to death when he was made pope. The Polish pope unsettled the Soviets during his state visit to Poland in June 1979, as the tectonic plates of Soviet Communism started to move away from Leningrad.

Then on May 13, 1981, the Feast of Our Lady of Fatima, Pope John Paul II was shot in St. Peter's Square. After he recovered from surgery, he requested that the third part of the Fatima secret be brought to him to read again. What it contained, written down by Lúcia decades before, detailed the murder of a bishop in white. John Paul was confident that he was this bishop, but miraculously, he was not killed.

After the assassination attempt, John Paul II was more determined than ever to consecrate Russia to Fatima as Our Lady had asked. Previous popes had tried and failed for various reasons—some political and others logistical. It was no easy task to bring all the bishops of the world together. Finally, in 1984, the consecration of Russia was carried out. Five short years later, the long-impenetrable Iron Curtain and the stalwart Soviet empire fell with a whimper. That the end of the empire did not involve massive bloodshed was a miracle in itself. The fact that it happened on Christmas day, 1991, makes Our Lady's role all the more pronounced.

Our Lady of Kazan Resurfaces

While it's still not clear what happened to the icons of Our Lady of Kazan in 1917, one of the icons resurfaced in 1953, when it was purchased by American F. A. Mitchell-Hedges. It was displayed in New York at the World Trade Fair in 1964–65. In 1970, the Blue Army of Our Lady of Fatima purchased the icon from Anna Mitchell-Hedges for $125,000 and enshrined it in Fatima, Portugal. Then in 1993, the icon was given to Pope John Paul II, who kept it close to him in his study, venerating it for eleven years. He said, "It has found a home with me and has accompanied my daily service to the Church with its motherly gaze."[13] After years of having an official papal visit to Russia blocked by the Moscow patriarchate, John Paul presented the icon to the Russian Church as an unconditional gift when it became

---

13   Bridget Curran, *The Miracles of Mary: Everyday Encounters of Beauty and Grace* (Crows Nest, Australia: Allen & Unwin, 2008), 37.

clear that, given his age and infirmity, he would never visit Russia. On July 21, 2005, the holy image was enshrined at the Annunciation Cathedral of the Kazan Kremlin.

Not the End

The story of Fatima is not yet over. The leaders in Russia have clearly spread more lies, and there are still one billion people living under Communism in China and millions more in Vietnam, Cuba, Laos, and North Korea. This chapter will have to remain unfinished until history unfolds and we see how Our Lady, as she promised at Fatima, will ultimately triumph over the great scourge of Communism.

PART III

Who Is This Woman?

CHAPTER 7

Mariolotry or Mariology?

As a young man, Karol Wojtyła's devotion to Mary grew significantly during the Second World War under the guidance of a devout layman (who will be discussed in chapter 13). Years later, the future pope confessed that he harbored reservations about how much attention to give to the Virgin. "At one point," Wojtyła wrote, "I began to question my devotion to Mary, believing that, if it became too great, it might end up compromising the supremacy of the worship owed to Christ."

As Wojtyła makes clear, there is something of an internal struggle that exists for many Christians about how much or how little to honor Mary. On one extreme, there are those who turn their devotion to Mary into something like goddess worship, neglecting her Son entirely while placing her into a more "spiritual" box. On the opposite extreme, there are those who dismiss her altogether, seeing her as simply another figure in a nativity scene. Over the centuries, the Church has responded to this tug-of-war. Pope Paul VI addressed it directly in his encyclical *Marialis*

Cultus. Before looking at that, however, it is important to grasp the types of veneration and worship—even if they might not be able to articulate it as such—commonly held among the faithful.

Layers of Veneration and Worship

Although not well known, over the centuries, an explanation has emerged about the different types of veneration and worship appropriate to those who are holy—namely, to the saints, angels, Mary, and the Trinity. The three layers are *dulia*, *hyperdulia*, and *latreia*. Instead of looking at worship and veneration as a binary option—either you worship something or you don't—early Christians saw that there are different ways, or layers, of honor. The first layer, dulia, is reserved for the veneration of men and women, or very holy men and women—those who became saints. Hyperdulia is still just reserved for humans, but this type is specifically geared toward venerating Mary because of her unique role in salvation history and as the Mother of God. The third kind of veneration, latreia (it is also spelled *latria*), is in actuality worship; it is giving to God what is due to Him as God. It is the highest form, reserved only for the Trinity, and does not include mere humans. It has a very precise meaning according to the old Greek term, entailing some kind of worship at an altar or some sort of sacrificial worship. These fine distinctions, while they might seem trivial, are important because of the way they animate the spiritual life of the faithful and provide guidance on the right relationship we should have to the holy.

Common Distortions of Marian Devotion

There is no question that goddess worship is a real thing (even if goddesses aren't), cropping up repeatedly throughout the centuries. Worshiping goddesses dates back in recorded history to ancient Greek and then Roman mythology. Athena, Aphrodite, Venus, Gaia, Juno, and Minerva are just a few of these figures. Even the Aztecs worshipped the goddess Tonantzin, who was honored on Tepeyac Hill before Our Lady of Guadalupe appeared there to Juan Diego. Many have mistakenly conflated the honor given to Mary as this same kind of worship, calling it "Mariolotry."

This sort of mistaken view is easy to find on vaguely spiritual websites and in books that argue that honoring Mary is just an extension of the goddess worship of old.[1] Recently, there was even a heresy out of the Philippines that was stomped out, called the Mary is God movement.

As the Church has made clear from the beginning, Mary isn't to be worshiped. She is not divine, but in her humanity perfected through grace, she always directs our deepest longings, petitions, and praises to her Son—the true God. Her deferment to Jesus is expressed most beautifully in Juan Diego's miraculous tilma. The Aztecs who looked upon the image would have "read" that by her bowed head, she herself was not a goddess but a powerful woman who deferred to God. Sadly, like weeds spouting up in freshly tilled soil,

---

1   See Susan Caperna Lloyd, *No Pictures on My Grave: A Spiritual Journey to Sicily* (Berkeley, CA: Mercury House, 1992), which conflates Mary with goddess worship.

these sorts of misunderstandings and misinterpretations of Mary are legion.

Christian Confusion

Amid the Christian landscape today, the Virgin Mary is still something of a lightning rod. The debate about what role Mary should play in the Church and how much we should honor her is long, heated, and sadly unresolved in many pockets of Christianity—particularly when no distinctions are made between veneration and worship.

Grappling with the role of Mary is nothing new. In the fifth century, the Church struggled to understand her relationship to Jesus. Was she simply the mother of Jesus in body only—as Nestorius, the bishop of Constantinople, argued—or was she really the Mother of God? Ultimately, the Church declared in 431 at the Council of Ephesus that Nestorius and his heresy were mistaken and that Mary is the Mother of God, *Theotokos*. Later, the second Marian dogma of her perpetual virginity was proclaimed at the Council of the Lateran in 649.

In the Eastern Churches, Mary is best known and honored through the title Theotokos, "Mother of God." Interestingly, however, Mariology stopped developing in those Eastern Churches not united to Rome following the Great Schism of 1054, which divided the Eastern and Roman Churches. As we will see, in the East, Mary is honored with a different sort of Rosary, and she is given tremendous honor in their liturgy, art, and architecture, but they do not accept the Roman Church's declaration of her immaculate conception (made dogma in 1854) or the assumption of Mary into heaven (made dogma in 1950). It can be argued that the Eastern Churches were the first to say, "We have gone far enough in our homage to Our Lady and need go no further." These dogmas continue to be a sticking point in ecumenical dialogue between the Eastern and Western Churches.

The debate over the Immaculate Conception—which was commonly held in the early Church dating back to St. Ephrem in fourth-century Syria and St. Augustine in the fifth century—was long and arduous. The debate was finally settled through medieval philosophy. As we saw in chapter 3, the "subtle doctor," Blessed John Duns Scotus—the source behind the "dunce cap" because his subtlety irritated his teachers, not because he was a dunce—is credited with finally articulating how it is that the Immaculate Conception happened. The debate highlights another significant difference between the East and the West that has only been exacerbated by the 1054 schism—namely, the reliance on philosophy and logic in the Roman tradition that pushed the boundaries of what is known about Mariology and other theological issues.

While the Eastern Church remained content with their understanding of Mary, the Protestant Reformation in the sixteenth century brought with it something categorically different. The theology of Martin Luther opened the door to stripping down the Christian faith to the barest of bones—*sola scriptura, sola fide*, "only the Bible, only faith." No more purgatory; no more tradition; no more sacraments; no more religious; no more feasts and fasts, liturgy and catechesis; and especially no more Rosary. What Luther did was open the door to a scorched earth policy about Mary, even if Lutherans themselves are not allergic to Mary. (Many Lutheran churches bear her name—they are more akin to the Eastern Orthodox insofar as they recognize her perpetual virginity and that she is the Mother of God.) Those who came after Luther just kept hacking away at the necessities of faith, leaving believers with little more than Bibles and few resources to interpret the deeply Catholic book (it was the Catholic Church that compiled the books of the Bible). Mary, Marian art, and Marian devotions were simply discarded with everything else that hinted at smells and bells.

In Reformation England, as the country was rocked by Henry VIII's decision to break with Rome and start his own Church of England over his adulterous marriage to Anne Boleyn, bonfires were held to rid the country of any Marian influence because her images were considered "too popeish." Madonna after Madonna went up in smoke. Mary was no longer needed within the realm of Christianity. She was demoted to simply window dressing, paraded out only for the Christmastime crèche because, well, someone has to hold the Baby Jesus.

Protestants generally became allergic to any type of honor for Mary, and that allergy lingers today. Contemporary debates show that the Protestant antidevotion to Mary is still alive and well. Recently, one Lutheran pastor described what happened when he hung images of Christ's life in his church that included Our Lady, such as Mary holding Jesus after He is taken off the Cross. The pastor was promptly told that the images were too Catholic and should be removed. For most Christians, the main issue boils down to this struggle: By honoring Mary, am I dishonoring Christ? After all, Christ is the one savior, while Mary is just His mother.

Protestants aren't the only ones who struggle with how to honor her, as we saw previously with Wojtyła. In 1950, when the dogma of Mary's assumption was proclaimed by Pope Pius XII, many suggested that the new dogma was driving a wedge deep into ecumenical dialogue. Many inside and outside the Church thought the pope had gone too far by making the Assumption a dogma—they felt that proclaiming it was simply not necessary. Again, at the root of the disagreement, those who objected to the dogma believed that it honored Mary too much.

Feminism, of course, has added its own twist on this debate. One feminist Catholic writer has suggested that Mary in medieval France was merely a reaction to legalistic male clergy, pitting Mary and priests against each other. Others have suggested that the old notion of Mary is simply too outdated, and no modern woman can relate to her. As a result, hymns, art, statuary, and so on should all be restructured to accommodate the "new" contemporary view of Mary—minus obedience, docility, and meekness.

Even in mainstream Catholic circles, Mariology has been reduced to trying to see Mary through a more human lens, such as a believer, disciple, or friend, minus deeper theological strings. Few Catholics in the pews know of her relationship to the Church, the rich understanding of her as the spouse of the Holy Spirit, or what it means to be "full of grace" as the Mother of God.

The real low point in Marian devotion and Mariological development among Catholics has been pinpointed at 1966–72. This certainly shouldn't be surprising, given the cultural chaos of those years following massive civil and

ecclesial upheaval in the wake of the Second Vatican Council, the arrival of "the pill," and the smoldering Cold War,
made hot in Vietnam. This is part of the reason too many
Catholics know too little about her and her significant role
in the Church. Mary has become untethered from the rich,
fruitful, and beautiful teachings about her that have punc-
tuated the work of saint after saint over the centuries, dating
back to the apostles and the catacombs.

Research on Mary, however, paints an interesting picture.
Those who believe she holds too large a place in theology are
generally linked to some kind of heterodoxy, heresy, or ideology that does not uphold the true teachings of the Church.
On the other hand, those who see that honoring her in ways
that are not inimical to the Faith quite often have been
named saints by the Church. One can find people who are
not canonized speak of the greatness of Mary, but you would
be hard pressed to find a canonized saint who spoke ill of
her. Critics will say that this is a self-serving argument, but
those who are truly interested in becoming saints and join-
ing the Son of God in heaven know that the best way to do
so is by honoring His mother. As St. Louis de Montfort said,
Mary "is the safest, easiest, shortest and most perfect way of
approaching Jesus."[2]

Defensor Mariae

The defenders of Mary are abundant and span the ages.
Countless books have been written about her. One of the

---

2   St. Louis de Montfort, *True Devotion to Mary* (Charlotte, NC:
      TAN Books, 2010), 56.

best known, *True Devotion to Mary* by St. Louis De Mont-fort, was hidden in a trunk only to be discovered centuries later. Lesser-known works have been written by Blessed Alan de Roche, St. Alphonsus Liguori, and more recently Arch-bishop Fulton Sheen. While at times some of these works can feel over the top or saccharine-y to our contemporary ears, they always reward the effort to read them if we can "adjust our ear" to the context of their time and sift out the eternal truths.

For the defenders of Mary who honor her not as a goddess but as a woman who has been honored by God (hyperdulia, as explained previously), their explanation of what Catholics ought to do is very simple: Jesus came to us through Mary; it is only right that we return to Him through her as well. As the eighteenth-century Mariol-ogist Father Chaminade said, "we do not go to Mary as our God, but we go to God through Mary, as faith tells us He came to us through her."[3] Jesus' whole life, from Mary's first "yes" until His ascension into heaven, has Mary as a central figure. To eliminate her from Scripture is to deform the story—to not tell it correctly—and actually dis-honors Jesus. Consider how much the common man hon-ors his own mother. How much more so does a perfect Man honor His perfect mother? Certainly not through neglect but also not through worship, which is a distortion of what

---

3   John M. Samaha, "William Joseph Chaminade's Contribution to Mariology," *International Marian Research Institute*, https://www.udayton.edu/imri/mary/w/william-joseph-chaminades-contribution-to-mariology.php.

the Church has always known Mary to be: human. But as the Mother of God and a woman created with the fullness of grace, she ought to be honored.

When we come to Mary, she brings us to Christ; whenever she is honored, Christ is honored. As Pope Paul VI pointed out, "the sun will never be dimmed by the light of the moon."[4] Barring the extremes of sentimentality or divinization, Marian devotion is Christian worship, insofar as "it takes its origin and effectiveness from Christ, finds its complete expression in Christ, and leads through Christ in the Spirit to the Father."[5]

Wojtyła's own resolution about how much to honor Mary was resolved by reading St. Louis de Montfort's *True Devotion*: "There I found the answers to my questions, Yes, Mary does bring us closer to Christ; she does lead us to him, provided that we live her mystery in Christ."[6] The Holy Father later added, "I understood that I could not exclude the Lord's Mother from my life without neglecting the will of God-Trinity, who willed to begin and fulfill the great mysteries of the history of salvation with the responsible

4   Pope Paul VI, "St. Maximilian Kolbe's Beatification Homily," *The Holy See*, October 17, 1971, https://w2.vatican.va/content/paul-vi/it/homilies/1971/documents/hf_p-vi_hom_19711017.html. Translated from Italian: *come non mai sarà oscurato il sole dalla luna*.

5   Pope Paul VI, introduction to *Marialis Cultus*, February 2, 1974, https://www.ewtn.com/library/PAPALDOC/P6MARIAL.HTM.

6   Gretchen Filz, "The Saint Who Influenced Pope Saint John Paul II's Profound Devotion to Mary," *GetFeed*, April 27, 2016, https://www.catholiccompany.com/getfed/true-devotion-mary-pope-john-paul-ii.

and faithful collaboration of the humble handmaid of Nazareth."[7] Like Cardinal Mindszenty before him, the future
pope saw that "veneration of Mary belongs of necessity to
Christianity, as Christ belongs to it. For Mother and Child
cannot be separated."[8]

One of the most referenced quotes in response to the
claim that Mary has been given too much credit comes to us
from Pope St. John XXIII, who is reputed to have said, "The
Madonna is not pleased when she is put above her son."[9]
What's missing is the context of this quote (which, unfortunately, I haven't been able to locate), and here the Holy
Father is likely referring to those who place Mary above
Christ or even dismiss Him as she is given the status of a
goddess. The Church is aware that such abuses occur but
has warned, along with many saints, that genuine Marian
devotion always leads a devotee to a deeper relationship with
Christ.

Father Chaminade offered Christ as the model of how to
honor Mary. He wrote, "Can we really assert too much, do
too much, provided we do not declare her equal to the Divinity, provided we make a distinction between her worship and

---

7   "Pope Reveals Mary's Role in His Life," *Zenit*, November 1,
     2000, http://www.zeitun-eg.org/jp2.htm.
8   Joseph Mindszenty, *The Face of the Heavenly Mother* (New York:
     Philosophical Library, 1951), 85–86.
9   This is quoted in Graef, without a footnote, and other citations
     of it refer back to Graef. It is entirely possible that Pope John XXIII
     said this, but I haven't been able to find a source beyond Graef.
     Hilda Graef, *Mary: A History of Doctrine and Devotion* (Notre
     Dame, IN: Ave Maria Press, 2009).

that of the Divinity? What has God said of Mary? What has He done for her? He is our model."[10]

A deeper look at centuries of study about Mary reveal that her contemporary promoters are saying relatively little that is actually new; they are mostly repeating theological ideas and scriptural exegesis that have been said by saint after saint, starting as early as the patristic period of the Desert Fathers and the towering figure of St. Augustine. The medieval period developed the theological notions about Mary even further, allowing her to bloom in the capable minds of men like St. Bernard of Clairvaux, St. Anselm of Canterbury, Albert the Great, St. Thomas Aquinas, and Blessed Duns Scotus. Mary should be treated not like a hot potato but as the source of deep grace, insight, and Christian revelation.

Know Them by Their Fruit

One of the struggles of talking about Mary is that much of her defense relies on the testimony of those who have loved and served her, which draws critics to say that their arguments are circular or self-serving. One way out of this cycle is to use the Scripture-sanctioned technique of looking at the fruit that has come from Marian devotion. What is the fruit of Mary's ardent devotees?

As we see in Matthew's Gospel, "a tree is known by its fruit" (Mt 12:33). There is clear evidence in the lives of the

---

10 "William Joseph Chaminade in Vignettes and Cameos," *International Marian Research Institute*, https://www.udayton.edu/imri/mary/w/william-joseph-chaminade-in-vignettes-and-cameos.php#anchor6.

faithful that Marian devotion doesn't thwart a relationship with Christ; on the contrary, it facilitates it. She is the facilitator par excellence. Mary tethers her children to Christ, like any good mother would. She doesn't want any child to be lost. Much of the reason for this is because she was there at the foot of the Cross; she knows full well what it cost her Son to purchase eternal life for all of us. She doesn't want a drop of Christ's sacrifice to be in vain.

As Blessed John Henry Cardinal Newman has pointed out, "Son and Mother went together; and the experience of three centuries has confirmed their testimony, for Catholics who have honoured the Mother, still worship the Son, while Protestants, who now have ceased to confess the Son, began then by scoffing at the Mother."[11] Newman experienced this firsthand in post-Reformation England, but it is also clear that mainline Protestantism has lost much of its faith—particularly as it capitulates further with secular and godless cultural trends.

What Newman and others have recognized is that devotion to Mary doesn't mean passivity; rather, her "spiritual motherhood promotes a childlike docility and expectation with regard to her ability and authority to form us into other Christs."[12] Many of the saints have testified to the transformation that has taken place in their lives because of their devotion to her.

---

11   John Henry Newman, "The Glories of Mary for the Sake of Her Son," *Newman Reader*, http://www.newmanreader.org/works/discourses/discourse17.html.

12   Johann G. Roten, "Marian Devotion for the New Millennium," *Marian Studies* 51 (2000): 58, http://ecommons.udayton.edu/marian_studies/vol51/iss1/7.

What Is Lost Without Her

There are many indiscernible details of what is lost when Marian devotion is absent. However, one visible societal element that has been lost is the proper understanding of women and their role in Protestant churches. Professor Catherine Tzacz talks about her experience studying with some Lutheran women and their surprise at the centrality that women play in Eastern Orthodox liturgy. The Protestant Reformation unwittingly erased many of the places where feminine spirituality—a spirituality profoundly different from masculine spirituality—flourished: "The Reformers, Patricia Ranft has shown, attacked institutions within Christianity that fostered women's visibility and high status, specifically monasticism, saints, and Mariology."[13] One commentator went so far as to suggest that "the Protestant rejection of the veneration of Mary and its various consequences (such as the really 'male-dominated' Protestant worship, deprived of sentiment, poetry and intuitive mystery-perception) is one of the psychological reasons which explains the recent emergence of institutional feminism."[14] Without giving women an authentic outlet for their fundamental need to worship and the unique way they go about doing it, Protestantism has pushed them in another direction—that is, eyeing those roles previously

---

13   Quoted in Catherine Brown Tzacz, "Women and the Church in the New Millennium," *St. Vladimir's Theological Quarterly* 52, no. 3–4 (2008): 243–74.

14   The Orthodox Church (September 1975): 4, cited by Bishop Kallistos Ware, "Man, Woman, and the Priesthood of Christ," in *Man, Woman and Priesthood* (London: SPCK, 1978), n. 25.

reserved for men because the feminine roles have been decimated. This argument has been made among Protestants themselves. Blogger and Lutheran Army chaplain Graham Glover wrote,[15]

> And it is my belief that those Christians who ignore and even reject the importance of the Blessed Mother do so to their theological detriment. Their ignorance is the cause of more theological problems than they realize. Their rejection is met with a radicalism they have no means to combat.[16]

> And without Mary being honored and revered on a regular basis by Christians, how can we possibly expect to know the fullness of God's truth? If we reject even the smallest element of God's revelation (and the Blessed Virgin is no small element!), we are setting ourselves and our churches up for complete and utter theological failure. We are begging for radical feminism, as well as other distortions of the faith, to become the norm.[17]

Glover rightly points out that not only does the abandonment of Mary damage the faith of women, but because Mary is no small part of the Christian story, Protestants have set themselves up for theological failure.

---

15   Tzacz, "Women and the Church."
16   Graham Glover, "Christianity's Radical Feminism Is Its Ignorance of the Blessed Mother," *Jagged Word*, August 12, 2015, https://thejaggedword.com/2015/08/12/christianitys-radical-feminism-is-its-ignorance-of-the-blessed-mother.
17   Ibid.

Others have warned Catholics against forgetting this Marian dimension of the Church (which we will soon discuss further). In the early 1970s, a French monk warned others not to emphasize the masculine over the feminine (or Marian) gifts of the Church because it would come at the expense of everyone: "All men, and especially members of the hierarchy, should make every effort to exclude from their mentality any sentiment of pride and superiority which is far from the spirit of the gospel and will end up provoking in women by way of reaction their desire to copy men and to disown the spiritual riches of the feminine world."[18] It seems, however, that the die was already cast because the women in the priesthood movement, despite repeated statements by popes, still lingers. Meanwhile, women are left with an anemic understanding of the unique spirituality they have been given, and therefore, they are left with a stunted faith and fulfillment of mission.

Rod Dreher has rightly pointed out that if Christians actually lived their faith, the world would not be in the situation it is now. Marian devotion stems the tide of heterodoxy, lukewarmness, and heresy. Devotion to Mary, as we have seen, has been indispensable in the clashes of civilizations over the centuries. The Church continues to recommend her to the faithful. The Second Vatican Council stated explicitly, "The Church experiences her help unceasingly, she recommends to the hearts of the faithful that they turn to Mary's patronage, so that her motherly help and protection may

---

18   André Feuillet, *Jesus and His Mother* (Petersham, MA: St. Bede's Publication, 1984), 214.

lead them all to be ever more closely united to the Mediator and Savior, Christ."[19]

Many of the very things that have been abandoned by Protestant Christians—such as "the papacy, the Holy Sacrifice of the Mass, Confession, priests, the intercession of the Virgin Mary, the rosary, and the confraternities"— were the keys in saving Christian Europe from the threats of Islam, atheism, and Communism, as we saw in previous chapters.[20] Now is certainly not the time to abandon these timeless treasures. We must take them up again with greater resolution, trust, and fervor.

---

19   Pope Paul VI, *Lumen Gentium*, November 21, 1964, #62, *The Holy See*, http://www.vatican.va/archive/hist_councils/ii _vatican_council/documents/vat-ii_const_19641121 _lumen-gentium_en.html.

20   Donald Calloway, *Champions of the Rosary* (Stockbridge, MA: Marian Press, 2016), 77.

CHAPTER 8

Mary and the Trinity

It Is All About Relationships

In St. Matthew's Cathedral in Washington, DC, there is a magnificent statue of Our Lady on the left side of the nave. She is not standing serenely; instead, her posture is one of action frozen in time—it captures the very act of her bridging the gap between heaven and earth. She is bending down, her right hand extended as if she is reaching for humanity, while her left hand is reaching up to heaven. Even the marble folds in her garments suggest movement. I've always been drawn to this statue, first because it is so unusual but, more important, because it concretizes what Mary wants to do for us every second of the day—connect us with God, whether it is through our prayers, our sacrifices, or even our brokenness. In short, she mediates for us.

Many years ago, I was blessed to have Father James Flanagan, the founder of the Society of Our Lady of the Most Holy Trinity (SOLT), as a spiritual director. He was a saintly man with an intimate closeness to Our Lady. One of the phrases he used so frequently during our conversations that I still hear ringing in my ears was, "It is all about *relationships*."

He wasn't talking about community living or building a family but about understanding the nature of God. The first and most fundamental relationship, he would explain, is found in the Trinity. In fact, the very existence of the third person of the Trinity, the Holy Spirit, was due to the relationship between the Father and the Son. As we say in the Nicene Creed each Sunday, the Holy Spirit "proceeds from the Father and the Son." From their love "came forth" (proceeds) a third person. And when we have that third person residing in our hearts, we can be assured that the love the Father and the Son have for each other is coursing through us.

Father Flanagan also spoke clearly about the role of Mary, our mother. Everything we needed to know about her, he stressed again, was understood within the bonds of *relationship*—her relationship to the Father, her relationship to the Son, her relationship to the Holy Spirit, and her relationship to the Church. Each relationship was unique, essential, and fruitful. Without understanding these, Mary is simply incomprehensible.

The relationship Mary has with the Trinity and the Church is packed up tidily in Luke 1:35: "And the angel answering, said to her: The Holy Ghost shall come upon thee, and the power of the Most High shall overshadow thee. And therefore also the Holy which shall be born of thee shall be called the Son of God." In two concise sentences, the mystery of the Trinity and the way it is woven into Mary's life are made clear in the simplest of terms. As we have seen over and over again, simple doesn't mean superficial, and there are great depths to be plumbed when it comes to Mary, the Trinity, and the Church. At the heart of these relationships is Mary as the link between heaven and earth, between the Trinity—the one God in three persons—and the created Church on earth. She is, as St. Bernardine of Sienna explained, the neck connecting the head to the body. Mary "is the neck of Our Head, by which He communicates to His mystical body all spiritual gifts."[1] She links heaven and earth.

The relationships between Mary and each person of the Trinity reflect on a very human level the natural relationship we find within a family, such as father, mother, spouse, son, and daughter, minus every sort of distortion that comes from sin. These relationships go well beyond the best possible relationships that we can imagine.

God in His goodness has given us an everyday icon in the family—father, mother, child—to help us comprehend His own inner life and the life the Trinity has with Mary. Entire books have been written on this. Even talking about the unique relationships that Mary has with each member of the Trinity is challenging because there is so much overlap with the other members. For example, it is impossible to explain the fruitfulness of Mary and the Holy Spirit without understanding the fruit—namely, Christ. And while it is possible to make these distinctions in our minds, in reality, these relationships are so tight, they cannot be separated.

Mary and the Father

Mary is the masterpiece of God the Father. "Throughout history," Pope Francis explained, "interwoven with the divine

---

1   St. Bernadine of Sienna, *Quadrag. de Evangel. Aetern, Serm*, x., a. 3, c. iii.

thread, is also a 'Marian thread' . . . Mary is that space, preserved free from sin, where God chose to mirror himself. She
is the stairway God took to descend and draw near to us."[2]

Planned from the beginning, Mary is foreshadowed
throughout the Old Testament. We can see her in phrases
such as Isaiah 7:14: "Therefore the Lord himself shall give
you a sign. Behold a virgin shall conceive, and bear a son,
and his name shall be called Emmanuel." We can also see
her foreshadowed in archetypes found in the Old Testament,
such as Rebecca, who helped Jacob secure his father's blessing, or Queen Esther, who saved her people from destruction by courageously appealing to the king.

In the fullness of time, God the Father saw fit to intro-
duce this woman into the world, full of grace and without
even the slightest stain of sin on her soul. In practical terms,
this means that Mary experienced no internal conflict over
her own will and God's will—they both are the same. For
centuries, she has been called the New Eve because she
reverses the damage done by Eve; Eve's disobedience is set
aright by Mary's act of obedience.

One of the radical struggles that many people have with
Mary is that they see her role as unnecessary because Christ's
sacrifice fulfills every requirement of salvation. Yes, Christ's sacrifice does fulfill every requirement for salvation, but there is
more to it than that. A narrow view of Scripture and theology
overlooks the very work and will of God the Father. God has

---

2   Diane Montagna, "Pope Francis: Mary Is 'The Stairway God
     Took to Descend and Draw Near to Us,'" *Aleteia*, July 28, 2016,
     http://aleteia.org/2016/07/28/pope-francis-mary-is-the
     -stairway-god-took-to-descend-and-draw-near-to-us/#sthash
     .D4dbebay.dpuf.

created His masterpiece, Mary, to prepare the world for His Son. This is how God has chosen to work in the world; He comes through Mary. Our God is an unchanging God, and so He will always come through Mary. It is out of a super-abundance of love that Mary was created. God the Father is no minimalist, and He knew that His work of salvation would be more perfect if performed through a perfect woman.

Mary is the pure conduit through which God came to us, but that role hasn't ended. She is still the perfect conduit for Him to come to us, and we can return to Him. As Archbishop Fulton Sheen said so eloquently, "since men are unprepared for a revelation of the heavenly image of Love, which is Christ Jesus Our Lord, God, in His mercy, has prepared on earth an image of love that is not Divine but can lead to the Divine. Such is the role of His Mother. She can lift the fear, because her foot crushed the serpent of evil; she can do away with dread, because she stood at the foot off the Cross when human guilt was washed away and we were born in Christ."[3]

Certainly, God could have done things differently, but out of His abundance of love, He has given us Mary, the icon of His unconditional love.

Mary and Christ

There are few relationships so tender as that of a mother and her child. But we know there is something even more special about Mary and Jesus, about *this mother* and *this child*. As Pope Paul VI wrote so powerfully, "Mary, the New

---

3   Fulton J. Sheen, *The World's First Love*, 2nd ed. (San Francisco: Ignatius Press, 2010), 202.

Woman, stands at the side of Christ, the New Man, within whose mystery the mystery of man alone finds true light; she is given to us as a pledge and guarantee that God's plan in Christ for the salvation of the whole man has already achieved realization in a creature: in her."[4] Mary has a very specific role; as Archbishop Fulton Sheen says, "Her role is to prepare for Jesus."[5] Such a role, however, doesn't stop at birth but continues down through the ages. Mary is always coming first to prepare our hearts for her Son.

The Blessed Virgin Mary, St. Louis de Montfort explained, is so inseparable from Jesus "that it would be easier to separate light from the sun."[6] Even a quick look at Jesus' life reminds us that Mary was there at the most important and most prominent events, from Christ's conception, birth, and presentation, to His agony on the Cross. She was there through all that was joyful, luminous, sorrowful, and glorious. Pope Paul VI adds that "sharing as she did the thoughts and the secret wishes of Christ she may be said to have lived the very life of her Son. Hence nobody ever knew Christ so profoundly as she did, and nobody can ever be more competent as a guide and teacher of the knowledge of Christ."[7] Truly, no mother knew her son's heart more than Mary.

---

4   Pope Paul VI, *Marialis Cultus*, February 2, 1974, #57, *EWTN*, https://www.ewtn.com/library/PAPALDOC/P6MARIAL.HTM.
5   Sheen, *World's First Love*, 190.
6   St. Louis de Montfort, *True Devotion to Mary* (Charlotte, NC: TAN Books, 2010), n. 63.
7   Pope Paul VI, *Signum Magnum*, May 13, 1967, #7, *The Holy See*, http://w2.vatican.va/content/paul-vi/en/apost_exhortations/documents/hf_p-vi_exh_19670513_signum-magnum.html.

Mary and the Holy Spirit

Mary is the spouse of the Holy Spirit. It is a phrase we have heard so many times, and yet too few stop to consider exactly what that means and the depths of its significance. To combat this negligence, it can be helpful to look at the bond that exists between human spouses. If we look at couples who have been married for decades, they can finish each other's thoughts, anticipate the other's needs before they are voiced, and when one precedes the other in death, the other is often not far behind. If we take these human examples and map them onto Mary and the Holy Spirit, a better picture comes into view of their relationship. Among creatures made in God's image, the union brought about by spousal love is the most intimate of all. In a much more precise, interior, essential manner, the Holy Spirit lives in the soul of the Immaculata—in the depths of her very being.[8]

One unique element about Mary and her spouse is that the Holy Spirit is not materially available for us to understand Him. What Mary does, like a good human spouse does, is represent Him for us, or gives us a visual image of what He looks like. One theologian has said that Mary provides us with a concrete and human image of the Holy Spirit: "Thanks to Mary, we are gratified with a quasi-physical portrait of the Paraclete and a more specific and concrete understanding of his mysterious ways."[9] Like

---

8   Dwight P. Campbell, "The Holy Spirit and Mary," *Homiletic & Pastoral Review* (May 1993), https://www.catholicculture.org/culture/library/view.cfm?recnum=4270.

9   Johann G. Roten, "Marian Devotion for the New Millennium," *Marian Studies* 51, no. 7 (2000): 124.

the old married couple, their wills are so intertwined that it's difficult to know where the will of one stops and the other starts. The Holy Spirit and the Mother of God are inseparable; "the Spirit is present wherever Mary's action appears."[10]

As we saw in chapter 5, there is a concrete link between Our Lady and the Holy Spirit in their very natures as *immaculately conceived*; the Holy Spirit proceeds outside of time, and Our Lady is created in time. Mary, St. Maximilian Kolbe wrote, "is the most perfect expression by the Creator of created, fruitful love, intended by him to reflect or image the divine Person who is Uncreated Love, the Fruit of the love flowing eternally between the Father and the Son."[11] Mary is the human expression of the Holy Spirit's love.

When Mary was conceived without sin, she became, as Pius IX says, "the dwelling place of all [His] grace," and therefore, "the Holy Spirit enables her to reflect within her soul (with her freely-willed cooperation) the Holy Spirit's most essential attribute: love that is superabundantly fruitful."[12] As Kolbe says, "He makes her fruitful, from the very first instant of her existence, all during her life, and for all eternity."[13]

With all this, we can return again to the question of why God would do things this way. Kolbe explains:

---

10   André Feuillet, *Jesus and His Mother* (Petersham, MA: St. Bede's Publication, 1984), 210.

11   Campbell, "Holy Spirit and Mary."

12   Ibid.

13   Ibid.

> Just as the Son, to show us how great his love is, became a man, so too the third Person, God-who-is-Love, willed to show his mediation as regards the Father and the Son by means of a concrete sign. This sign is the heart of the Immaculate Virgin, according to what the saints tell us, especially those who love to consider Mary as the spouse of the Holy Spirit. This was the conclusion drawn by St. Louis de Montfort, in accordance with the teaching of the Father . . . Since the death of Christ, the Holy Spirit acts within us too, by means of Mary.[14]

To simplify, Mary is the icon of the unique type of love of the Holy Spirit. She manifests this love to us in concrete ways. The relationship between Mary and her spouse doesn't remain boxed in and unconnected to other relationships. The fruitfulness of one leads to the other. It leads, as it does in the natural world, to motherhood. As *Lumen Gentium* says, "she is a virgin who 'keeps whole and pure the fidelity she has pledged to her Spouse' and 'becomes herself a mother,' for 'she brings forth to a new and immortal life children who are conceived of the Holy Spirit and born of God.'"[15]

"All grace," says St. Maximilian Kolbe, "ultimately comes to us from God the Father, through the merits of Jesus

---

14   H. M. Manteau-Bonamy, *Immaculate Conception and the Holy Spirit: The Marian Teachings of St. Maximilian Kolbe*, 3rd ed. (Libertyville, IL: Marytown Press, 2008), 90–91.

15   Pope Paul VI, *Lumen Gentium*, November 21, 1964, #64, *The Holy See*, http://www.vatican.va/archive/hist_councils/ii _vatican_council/documents/vat-ii_const_19641121 _lumen-gentium_en.html.

Christ, His Son, and is distributed by the Holy Spirit; and the Holy Spirit, in distributing all grace, works in and through Mary."[16] Since Mary is this faithful spouse of the Holy Spirit, it is through her that all graces flow to earth. This is why she is continually called—especially by the Church, popes, St. Maximilian, and others throughout history—the mediatrix of all graces. This happens not out of necessity but again as a part of God the Father's loving plan of salvation: "God *wills* to do so. And God wills to do so for a reason: Jesus, the Source of all grace, came through Mary via the work of the Holy Spirit; therefore it is fitting that all grace continue to come through Mary by the work of the Holy Spirit."[17]

Mary and the Church

Somewhere in the last several hundred years, an odd separation of the inseparable developed in the minds of many of the faithful. Somehow the Church and Our Lady were placed on separate mental pages. Yes, there might be some overlap in that they are both referred to as "mother," but otherwise, the Church is monolithic and expansive, while Mary should be left to the side chapels or recitation of the Rosary after Mass, right? It's difficult to pinpoint why this divide happened, although much of it is likely connected to the Protestant Reformation and the subsequent excising of Mary from the theological picture. It is not difficult, however, to see the abundant evidence that this separation of Mary and the Church is deeply flawed.

---

16   Campbell, "Holy Spirit and Mary."
17   Ibid.

From the very beginning of the Church, "Mary and the Church are seen as one, for the Church had it's beginning in her womb, and from her virginal earth the kingdom of God has blossomed."[18] From the earliest days, Mary was understood as "a type or symbol of the Church, and therefore everything that we find in the Gospel about Mary can be understood in a proper biblical sense of the mystery of the Church."[19]

Mary is the model of discipleship and the eschatological fulfillment of what is to come: "In Mary the Church admires and extols the most excellent fruit of the Redemption; and in her as in a most pure mirror, the Church contemplates with joy what she herself desires and hopes to be."[20] So both show us how to follow her Son and provide a view of what Christ does through the Church—namely, perfects us to share in His love for eternity in heaven.

This overlap of the Church and Mary grows clearer when you see the characteristics of Mary applied to the Church: spotless, free from sin, a mother—Mary is the Virgin made Church, a phenomenon articulated in both the Western and the Eastern Churches. *Lumen Gentium* explains:

> The Church, moreover, contemplating Mary's mysterious sanctity, imitating her charity, and faithfully

---

18   Hugo Rahner, *Our Lady and the Church* (1951; repr., Stamullen, Ireland: Zaccheus Press, 2005), 11.

19   Ibid., 13.

20   Pope Paul VI, *Sacrosanctum Concilium*, December 4, 1963, #103, *The Holy See*, http://www.vatican.va/archive/hist _councils/ii_vatican_council/documents/vat-ii_const _19631204_sacrosanctum-concilium_en.html.

fulfilling the Father's will, becomes herself a mother by accepting God's word in faith. For by her preaching and by baptism she brings forth to a new and immortal life, children who are conceived of the Holy Spirit and born of God. The Church herself is a virgin, who keeps whole and pure the fidelity she has pledged to her Spouse. Imitating the Mother of her Lord, and by the power of the Holy Spirit, she preserves with virginal purity and integral faith, a firm hope and sincere charity.[21]

When most of us think of the Church, we think of St. Peter's Basilica, the Vatican, and the pope and priests. These elements embody the Petrine model of the Church. There is, however, a Marian element—which is just as critical—that is not in competition with the Petrine but acts in a complementary way. In fact, because of the spousal relationship between Mary and the Holy Spirit, "the Marian dimension gives the 'spirit' in which each pope carries out his specific service to the Church in its Petrine dimension."[22] Pope John Paul II spoke about these dual dimensions in the Church: "The Immaculate Mary precedes all others, including obviously Peter himself and the Apostles."[23] The Petrine, he argued, "presupposes the Church living out the Marian dimension. The Marian dimension

---

21 *Lumen Gentium*, #64.

22 Gary Devery, "Marian and Petrine Dimensions of the Church," http://www.clerus.org/clerus/dati/2003-04/01-999999/05ING.html.

23 Pope John Paul II, "The Marian and Petrine Principles" (annual address to the Roman Curia, December 22, 1987), http://www.piercedhearts.org/jpii/addresses_speeches/1997/marian_petrine_principles.htm.

forms a necessary substratum without which the Petrine dimension of the Church would be frustrated and limited in its fruitfulness."[24] It is for this reason that the Church limps so terribly when we neglect Mary and the Marian dimension of the Church. The Marian is *essential*.

"This link between the two profiles of the Church," the Polish pope continues, "the Marian and the Petrine, is profound and complementary. This is so even though the Marian profile is anterior not only in the design of God but also in time, as well being supreme and pre-eminent, richer in personal and communitarian implications for individual ecclesial vocations."[25]

Pope Leo XIII, followed by Pope Paul VI, declared Mary the "Mother of the Church." By doing this, they made explicit what has been known in the Church from the very beginning. And because of this inseparable relationship between Mary and the Church, one cannot love one without the other. St. Chromatius of Aquileia observed, "The Church was united . . . in the Upper Room with Mary the Mother of Jesus and with His brethren. The Church therefore cannot be referred to as such unless it includes Mary the Mother of our Lord, together with His brethren."[26]

Mary and the Devil

There is one more relationship we can consider to get a full picture of Mary: the *via negativa*—that is, her relationship

---

24 Devery, "Marian and Petrine Dimensions."
25 Ibid.
26 *Marialis Cultus*, #28.

to the Devil. There is much to be said about who one's enemies are. Since the beginning in Genesis, we are told about the enmity that will exist between "the woman" and the serpent: "I will put enmities between thee and the woman, and thy seed and her seed: she shall crush thy head, and thou shalt lie in wait for her heel" (Gn 3:15). Of course, the woman isn't referring to Eve but to the New Eve, Mary.

Father Gabriele Amorth, who was the Vatican's exorcist for years until his passing in 2016, spoke often about invoking Mary during exorcisms. "The demon is terrified of her," he wrote in a book published just after his death. He continued, "In order to be very clear, I wish to cite an episode at which I personally assisted many years ago. During an exorcism, Father Candido asked the devil a question: 'Why are you more afraid when I invoke Mary than when I implore God Himself?' He responded: 'I feel more humiliated being conquered by a simple creature than by God Himself.'"[27]

What Father Amorth experienced goes back to a basic theological principle: God confounds the proud through the humble. Mary, a human woman, humiliates the proud. As Blessed Columba Marmion—a nineteenth-century Irish priest, prolific spiritual author, and Abbot—said, "the ways of God are entirely different from our ways. To us it seems necessary to employ powerful means in order to produce great effects. This is not God's method; quite the contrary.

---

27   Gabriele Amorth, *An Exorcist Explains the Demonic* (Manchester, NH: Sophia Press, 2016), 123.

He likes to choose the weakest instruments that He may confound the strong."[28]

As ever, Mary remains the humblest human to have ever lived, and yet through her, heaven and earth are brought together, and Satan is crushed. Not bad for a simple Jewish girl.

28   Paul A. Zalonski, "Blessed Columba Marmion," *Tag Archives*, October 3, 2016, http://communio.stblogs.org/index.php/tag/columba-marmion.

CHAPTER 9

Mary's Maternal Care on a Personal Level

Up to this point, most of our discussion about Mary has centered on her role as military genius and cultivator of culture. We have also approached her in theological terms. As St. Juan Diego reminds us, while she is many things, Mary is also our "little mother." And her relationships do not stop at the Trinity. Whether we know it or not, we live in relationship with her daily; some are just more aware of it than others, taking time to cultivate it and help it grow deeper.

Mary is our tender mother who, like any good mother, anticipates our needs long before we're even aware of them. Mary is the most perfect mother imaginable, and therefore, she helps us with basic and spiritual needs, she brings order to our lives, she comforts us, and she encourages us.

Mary's maternity for the world started at the foot of the Cross at Calvary. There, her maternal care toward her Son manifests its ecclesiological dimension when it is extended to the whole Church. John, representing the community of disciples, is called to accept Mary, and the Church, as a mother.[1] "A mother becomes more attached to a child, the more suffering he has cost her," French theologian Father Feuillet explained. "It was in the trial of the Annunciation and the terrible sufferings of Golgotha that Mary brought forth humanity to the supernatural life."[2] While many believe that Mary did not labor in pain at the birth of Christ, it is clear that she labored dramatically for the birth of His Church at the foot of the Cross for her spiritual children. In the way Eve was able to give humanity human life, Mary, the New Eve, has given us spiritual life. But her obligation didn't end there: "As the Mother of life and of grace, she has given us life and daily supplies our souls with the graces that must nourish them, strengthen them, and bring them to the fullness of perfect maturity. For it is from her bounty that we receive all the help we need for our salvation."[3] And she performs her tasks thoroughly, as we have seen in previous chapters. She is ever "watching over all Christians, her children, with the most tender solicitude, fulfilling in their behalf the sublime duties of a

---

1   Gary Devery, "Marian and Petrine Dimensions of the Church," http://www.clerus.org/clerus/dati/2003-04/01-999999/05ING .html.

2   André Feuillet, *Jesus and His Mother* (Petersham, MA: St. Bede's Publication, 1984), 208.

3   "William Joseph Chaminade in Vignettes and Cameos," *International Marian Research Institute*, https://www.udayton.edu/imri/ mary/w/william-joseph-chaminade-in-vignettes-and-cameos .php#anchor6.

Mother."[4] Perhaps more than anything, "Mary helps Christians understand with what tenderness they are embraced by God."[5]

Over the centuries, Mary has come to humanity under hundreds of titles; some represent places, while others represent her motherly attributes. These titles—as well as examples of individuals who have miraculously been on the receiving end of her graces—tell us a lot about who she is and what she longs to do for us, her beloved children.

Star of the Sea

The title "Star of the Sea," or *Stella Maris* in Latin, encompasses every sort of protection and assistance offered by Our Lady. This is an ancient title given to Mary through St. Jerome's Latin translation of her name from the original Greek in the fourth century. St. Bernard of Clairvaux was a particular advocate for this title of Mary's, recommending it often. He explained its efficacy and the breadth of things for which one should seek Mary's assistance: "When the storms of temptation encompass you, look up to this star, invoke Mary. When the waves of pride are washing over your ship, look up to this star, invoke Mary. When the burden of sin and the thought of judgment to come terrifies you, think of Mary. If you follow her, you will not go astray. And if you hold fast to her, you will not fail."[6] Other titles similar

---

4   Ibid.
5   Feuillet, *Jesus and His Mother*, 209.
6   Luigi Gambero, *Mary in the Middle Ages* (San Francisco: Ignatius Press, 2005), 140.

to Star of the Sea are Our Lady of Prompt Succor; Mary, Help of Christians; Our Lady of Perpetual Help; Our Lady of Good Remedy; and Our Lady Undoer of Knots.

The earliest-known prayer to Mary dates back to 250. Written in Greek, it was found on a fragment of papyrus. It refers to Mary as the Mother of God, which is significant because the Council of Ephesus, where Mary was declared Mother of God, wouldn't happen for two more centuries. The prayer reads as follows: "Beneath thy compassion, we take refuge, O Mother of God; do not despise our petitions in time of trouble, but rescue us from dangers, only pure one, only blessed one."[7] From the earliest days of the Church, the faithful have known that Mary is a great source of help.

Over the centuries, there are countless stories attesting to Mary's protection in times of danger; she has stopped plagues, fires, assaults, and wars. Father James Flanagan, founder of the Society of Our Lady of the Most Holy Trinity (SOLT), explained one miracle of protection that Our Lady performed in his life. During the Second World War, Flanagan was in the navy and part of the demolition crew charged with clearing the bombs on Omaha Beach on D-Day. Out of one hundred men in his unit—most of whom simply detonated the bombs with their bodies because there wasn't time to detonate them properly—only three survived. Father Flanagan recalled seeing Our Lady wrap her mantle around him to protect him from the bombs exploding nearby.

---

7   Daniel Esparza, "Let Us Pray: The Earliest Known Marian Prayer," *Aleteia*, July 8, 2016, http://aleteia.org/2016/07/08/let -us-pray-the-earliest-known-marian-prayer.

Another story took place in 1788, when New Orleans was engulfed in a citywide fire. The Ursuline nuns' convent faced imminent destruction, as the strong winds blew the fire toward the building. As the nuns evacuated, Sister St. Anthony placed a small statue of Our Lady of Prompt Succor in the window seat of the convent, facing the fire. She and Mother Michel began to pray, "'Our Lady of Prompt Succor, we are lost unless you hasten to our aid!' Immediately, the wind shifted direction, blowing the flames away from the convent allowing for the fire to be extinguished. The Ursuline convent was one of the few buildings spared from destruction."[8]

Perhaps one of the most moving stories of Our Lady's protection is the one told by Immaculée Ilibagiza, who survived the genocide in Rwanda. She recounts the harrowing details in her book *Left to Tell: Discovering God Amidst the Rwandan Holocaust*. During this genocide, the majority Hutu tribe massacred one million of their Tutsi neighbors, destroyed their once prosperous country, and shattered the lives of the survivors. Immaculée found shelter from the bloodthirsty Hutu gangs in the tiny bathroom of a compassionate Hutu pastor. For ninety-one days, she and several young girls were packed into the small room, with little space to move and a meager amount of food. On top of that, these girls lived with the fear that if discovered, they would be raped and hacked to death. The last thing Immaculée's father gave her was a

---

8   "Our Lady of Prompt Succor," *Wikipedia*, last modified January 7, 2017, https://en.wikipedia.org/wiki/Our_Lady_of _Prompt_Succor#cite_note-3.

rosary. She held onto it as if it were life itself. Crowded in that bathroom as her killers roamed around outside—even calling her name at one point—she found a great light in the midst of terrifying darkness. She emerged a different person, transformed by her intimate encounter with a loving God.

Immaculée survived with more than just her life, having developed a deep faith in the worst of circumstances. Sadly, her family and most of her friends perished. She knows the Rosary offered her a lifeline, both physically and spiritually, to deal with the terror, sadness, and devastation about which she lived to tell.

Mater Amabilis, Loving Mother

Another Marian title is *Mater Amabilis*, or "Loving Mother." Loving mothers look for the small stuff. While Mary is there for the big things, she also sees importance in minor details.

A dear friend of mine was moving into a new apartment in a new city. As she watched the movers and her friends clear out after all the boxes had been moved, she found herself feeling very alone, questioning her move. As she closed the front door of her new apartment, she found the most delicate rosary hanging on the handle. She knew her Mother was with her.

There is a folksy story told about the newly canonized St. Junípero Serra, one of the missionaries who worked up and down California in a chain of missions. On one of his trips, Father Serra and his traveling companion, Father Palóu, needed a place to stay overnight while on a thirty-two-day trip through desolate terrain. They were met by a man, his wife, and their child, who provided them a place to stay in their tiny but extremely tidy home. The following day, after thanking their gracious hosts, the two friars went on their way. They then happened upon a group of muleteers who said there wasn't a house or ranch for miles. Trying to convince them otherwise, the two friars returned to the site, only to find three cottonwoods that had sheltered the humble home.

They marveled at the experience, especially the cleanliness of the house despite its poverty, the affectionate tenderness of the hospitality they received, and the deep interior consolation they both felt while staying with this exceptional family. The friars concluded that their hosts had to have been the Holy Family.

Our Lady, Seat of Wisdom

Mary is also known as the Seat of Wisdom, given that she is the mother of Wisdom Incarnate, Christ. As such, she is the Destroyer of Heresies. The early centuries of the Church were rife with doctrinal heresies that were eventually defeated. For those that have yet to be defeated, the culpability can be laid at the feet of humanity and neglect and sinfulness in the face of so many warnings, messages, and apparitions.

However, among those who have helped defeat heresy, such as St. Dominic and St. Francis de Sales, devotion to Mary "brings purity to the soul and therefore clarity to the mind."[9] Through this inspiration, she not only stomps out

---

9   Paul Scalia, "Mary, Destroyer of All Heresies," *The Catholic Thing*, August 4, 2016, https://www.thecatholicthing .org/2016/08/14/mary-destroyer-of-all-heresies.

heresy but also inspires tight logic, deep intellectual insights, and creative forms of communication and rhetoric.

Archbishop Charles Chaput of Philadelphia, describing what has happened to Catholics culturally for the last several decades, recently reported, "If we want to reclaim who we are as a Church, if we want to renew the Catholic imagination, we need to begin, in ourselves and in our local parishes, by unplugging our hearts from the assumptions of a culture that still seems familiar but is no longer really 'ours.'"[10] The archbishop added that the "problem is that many U.S. Catholics have abandoned this 'spiritual struggle' and have assimilated too much into the popular culture 'that bleaches out strong religious convictions in the name of liberal tolerance and dulls our longings for the supernatural with a river of practical atheism in the form of consumer goods.'"[11]

What we need, the archbishop continued, is to "look to Mary to be part of a religion that fights for truth, rather than assimilating to the popular culture. 'This is why Mary—the young Jewish virgin, the loving mother, and the woman who punches the devil in the nose—was, is, and always will be the great defender of the Church.'"[12] Referencing a medieval illustration of Mary punching the Devil in the nose, Archbishop Chaput continued, "She doesn't rebuke him. She doesn't enter into a dialogue with him. She punches the devil in the nose." He added that such an illustration is apt

---

10   Matt Hadro, "Archbishop Chaput: Be like Mary; Punch the
      Devil in the Nose," *EWTN*, October 21, 2016, http://ewtnnews
      .com/catholic-news/US.php?id=14460#.WArfCzDwPls.
11   Ibid.
12   Ibid.

because, as C. S. Lewis has pointed out, "Christianity is a 'fighting religion'—not in the sense of hatred or violence directed at other persons, but rather in the spiritual struggle against the evil in ourselves and in the world around us, where our weapons are love, justice, courage and self-giving."[13] Mary, as the Seat of Wisdom, inspires all of this.

The Ark of Noah

Our Lady is well known for calming both storms and humanity. St. Alphonsus de' Liguori tells the story of a vision had by St. Gertrude where Mary appears with her mantle spread out, and under the folds of it are wild beasts. Not just tolerating the beasts, Mary welcomes them with delicate tenderness. Mary protects her children from beasts by subduing the beasts, taming them, and bringing order to them. After all, they, too, are God's creatures.

Beasts also figure into the Marian title of the Ark of Noah because she saves anyone from damnation who takes shelter in her. Like the beasts, good and bad, that were saved from the great rains, Our Lady saves those who come to her.

Additionally, Mary has tamed more than just animals. In Genesis 3:16, the Lord explains to Adam and Eve what their punishment will be for disobedience: "To the woman also he said: 'I will multiply thy sorrows, and thy conceptions: in sorrow shalt thou bring forth children, and thou shalt be under thy husband's power, and he shall have dominion over thee.'" This dominion of man over woman is not a perfection but a curse upon women for Eve's disobedience. We can

---

13   Ibid.

see this clearly in relationships where there is no striving for virtue; men use their brute force to control or enslave women, while in the opposite situation—where both male and female are recognized as God's children with an innate dignity—the respect between men and women looks more like what God intended in the garden: harmony, not homogeny or one diminishing the other. Mary's influence, however, helps correct these relationships and brings both men and women into the order of grace, similar to what was intended before the Fall. Art historian Sir Kenneth Clark remarked that Mary "taught a race of tough and ruthless barbarians the virtues of tenderness and compassion."[14]

Again, like the beasts, Mary doesn't just subdue men; she transforms them. Cardinal Mindszenty explains, "The man, formerly a tyrant and ruler over the woman, becomes a troubadour and servant of the lady now that the gospel has come into the world. The spiritual beauty which God's hand has caused to bloom in the dignity of motherhood holds man spellbound. Tyrannous sensuality gives way in woman's presence, because purity, sanctity, and a heavenly radiance encompass her."[15] All this arose with devotion to Mary. Certainly, women and childbearing were not new arrivals with Christianity, but Christ's incarnation in the womb of Mary reoriented the beauty of a woman's ability to bear a child in a way that reveals the dignity of motherhood.

---

14   Kenneth Clark, "Civilization," DVD series, BBC Production, 2006.
15   Joseph Mindszenty, *The Face of the Heavenly Mother* (New York: Philosophical Library, 1951), 89.

Finally, Mary has the profound ability to convert the seemingly inconvertible. In Moorish Spain, there were many miracles of men converting to Christianity. What is intriguing about these stories, however, is that they usually involve very scary imagery or situations—like angels with fiery swords—that provoke the conversion. The stories related to the women and children, however, are very sweet and gentle. Truly, Mary knows her audience and what each soul needs.

Mother of Mercy

A lot of attention has been given (rightfully) to the Divine Mercy devotion, propagated by St. Faustina Kowalska. Few are aware that the story does not just start with St. Faustina's engagements with Jesus in Vilnius, Lithuania. Daniel di Silva, producer of the film *The Original Image of Divine Mercy*, said that Mary figures greatly in the Divine Mercy story. He explained that centuries before Jesus appeared to St. Faustina in what is known as the city of mercy, Vilnius, the city was surrounded by protective walls, and the gate in and out of the city was called *Ostra Brama*, "The Gate of Dawn." The gate used to house the image of Our Lady of the Dawn to ward off attackers while also blessing travelers. In the 1600s, a proper chapel was built to house the image of Our Lady amid the wall. In 1702, the Swedes captured the city, but Vilnius was rescued by Our Lady's miraculous image. At a turning point in the war, the heavy iron gates of the wall fell unexpectedly, immediately crushing to death four Swedish soldiers. After that, the Lithuanian army launched a counterattack and was victorious. Love for the image swelled until it was renamed Mother of Mercy in 1927, well before the Divine Mercy apparitions started. Di Silva points out that, "like Bethlehem, Our Lady was there [in Vilnius] first, followed by Jesus."[16] The first place where the Divine Mercy image of Christ was displayed—painted through St. Faustina's direction based on the apparitions—was at the Ostra Brama Chapel in Vilnius.

In addition to the connection between the image of Our Lady of the Dawn and the Divine Mercy image, Mary has a strong presence in St. Faustina's diary. On the feast of Our Lady of Mercy, 1935, Mary spoke to St. Faustina about the link between her spiritual motherhood and Divine Mercy: "I am Mother to you all, thanks to the unfathomable mercy of God."[17]

St. Faustina speaks very vividly about Mary's protection as the Mother of Mercy. She writes, "Midst storms, 'tis you [Mary] who teach me to love the Lord, O my shield and my defense from the foe"[18] and "I am quite at peace, close to Her Immaculate Heart. Because I am so weak and inexperienced, I nestle like a little child close to Her heart."[19] Mariologist Father Donald Calloway (former runner for the Japanese mafia turned Catholic priest) points out that "in the mind of St. Faustina, the Immaculate Conception

16   Daniel Di Silva, phone conversation with the author, October 7, 2016.
17   Donald Calloway, *Purest of All Lilies* (Stockbridge, MA: Marian Press, 2008), 53, diary entry #449.
18   Ibid., 113.
19   Maria Faustina Kowalska, *Diary: Divine Mercy in My Soul* (Stockbridge, MA: Marian Press, 2005), diary entry #1097.

serves as a 'sturdy anchor,' 'shield,' 'protection,' and strength."[20]

Also in her diary, St. Faustina mentions the Mother of God, *Theotokos*, sixty-six times. What's interesting is that this title is the one preferred by the Eastern Orthodox Churches. It seems more than coincidental that she should use this term frequently, since the devotion was started in Lithuania and Poland—both countries on the seam between East and West. The diary seems to be purposefully using language that can be understood by both Lungs (East/West) of the Church.

While St. Faustina was writing her diary, another future saint was thinking about Mary's connection to Divine Mercy. St. Maximilian Kolbe explains, "St. Bernard says that the Lord God kept for Himself justice but gave mercy to the Mother of God. I don't deny that the Immaculate receives the mercy from the Lord God, but she is the personification of this divine mercy and that is why a soul is converted and sanctified if it turns to her."[21]

Archbishop Fulton Sheen, a decade or two after St. Faustina and Kolbe, also spoke of Mary's important role in mercy. Sheen said that the story of Esther "has been interpreted through the Christian ages as meaning that God will reserve to Himself the reign of justice and law, but to Mary, His Mother, will be given the reign of mercy."[22]

---

20   Calloway, *Purest of All Lilies*, 86.

21   Maximilian Kolbe, *Let Yourself Be Led by the Immaculate* (Kansas City: Angelus Press, 2013), Kindle ed., loc. 325.

22   Fulton J. Sheen, *The World's First Love*, 2nd ed. (San Francisco: Ignatius Press, 2010), 182.

Finally, Mary spoke directly to St. Bridget about what it means in practical terms for her to be Mother of Mercy: "I am the Queen of heaven and the Mother of Mercy. I am the joy of the just and the door through which sinners come to God. There are no sinners on earth so unfortunate as to be beyond my mercy. For even if they receive nothing else through my intercession, at least they receive the grace of being less tempted by the devils than they would otherwise be." Even after death, Our Lady explained, "unless the last irrevocable sentence [of damnation] has been pronounced against them, there are no persons so abandoned by God that they will not return to Him and find mercy, if they invoke my aid."[23] Here again, Our Lady reminds us that her mercy doesn't start with her, but with her Son: "I am called by all the Mother of Mercy. It is my Son's mercy toward human beings that has made me merciful too."[24]

Which Madonna?

As Christopher Columbus and his crew were returning home from their first voyage to the New World, a tremendous storm met them on the high seas. They prayed and prayed, finally deciding to draw lots with a marked garbanzo bean to see who would make a pilgrimage to Our Lady of Guadalupe (in Spain) as a way of asking Our Lady to calm the storm. Columbus drew the winning bean. But the storm did not abate. They repeated the drawing, this time for someone

---

23   Reprinted in St. Alphonsus Liguori, *The Glories of Mary* (1868; repr., Totowa, NJ: Catholic Book Publishing, 1991), 23.

24   Ibid.

to make a pilgrimage to Our Lady of Loreto. Still the storm blew on. Next, they chose a pilgrimage to the Church of St. Clara of Moguer, known to intercede for mariners. Still again, the storm continued. Amy G. Remensnyder writes, "In desperation, Columbus and the ship's crew abandoned all thoughts of particular Madonnas and simply invoked the universal Mary. They made a collective vow that, if they survived the storm, at their first landfall they would hasten in a solemn procession . . . to the nearest church of Our Lady."[25] With that, the seas grew calm, and the winds died down. The lesson, perhaps, was that despite all the glorious titles, Our Lady simply wants to be remembered as the universal Mary, God's mother.

25   Amy G. Remensnyder, *La Conquistadora* (London: Oxford University Press, 2014), 10.

CHAPTER 10

Anti-Mary or the Age of Mary?

Throughout history, there are particular eras that show thriving Marian devotion. Among them are thirteenth-century France, when St. Dominic propagated the Rosary and when the Gothic era of architecture was in full swing; fifteenth-century Italy, when Marian art and music were at their peak; thirteenth- through fifteenth-century Spain during the Reconquista and exploration periods; sixteenth-century Mexico in the afterglow of Our Lady of Guadalupe's conversions; and many centuries in Poland—particularly the twentieth century, when her assistance was so instrumental in ending Communism. There is very little today in our culture that resembles the glorious "ages of Mary" of the past. One could argue that not only are we not living in an age of Mary; we are living in anti-Mary times.

In writing this book, I was struck by the fact that in all of Mariology, there is no mention of a potential "anti-mary." While the idea of an antichrist has been batted about since St. John spoke of an "antichrist" in the first century (cf. 1 Jn 4:3; 2 Jn 1:7), there is no discussion about a spirit opposed to Our Lady. While this might seem like an odd suggestion, it doesn't seem so odd when one considers that Mary has long been called the New Eve, and Christ the New Adam. If Christ is the New Adam, and Mary the New Eve, it only makes sense that an antichrist would have the female complement of an antimary. In the same way that an antichrist can be an idea or a movement (and not just a person), an antimary can also be seen as a movement.

So just what might an anti-Mary movement look like? Well, for starters, it would embody Eve's vice of disobedience and her encouraging Adam to share in her disobedience. But such a movement would also, of course, capture the antithesis of Mary. Mary is not only obedient but also deeply receptive to the will of the Father, even when she doesn't completely understand it. She is meek and says little but holds significant sway. She is also patient, humble, persevering in suffering, and fiercely devoted to her Son and her spiritual children.

In this description, I have purposefully used language that sounds archaic to our ears without trying to spin the ideals of Mary into contemporary or more compelling terms. I did this for two reasons. First, some of these terms are apposite and not easily changed into different terms. For instance, *meek* is a difficult word to capture the whole meaning of with another word. Second, as you read these words, they might have struck you as very inaccessible. Women just aren't like this anymore, and for this reason, much of the contemporary research on Mary suggests that she needs to change—contemporary authors suggest that we need to adapt her to a more contemporary vision of womanhood. However, these authors don't realize that not only is something significant lost when we "adapt" Mary; something significant has been lost from our culture because we have "adapted" women. This chasm between the woman Mary was/is and the women we have become today shows just how deeply embedded the anti-Mary movement is in our culture. If we no longer recognize the goodness that was at the heart of women for millennia, then we need to ask ourselves what has happened and how we have gone so far astray in just a generation or two.

What is even more interesting is how difficult it is to have a conversation about this topic in the public square. It seems that unless women's every whim and fancy are being pushed through legislation or media, we aren't treating women fairly. If men dare to point out that perhaps women are missing something integral to their feminine nature, they are quickly castigated as sexist and/or stupid. The women who speak about this fair slightly better but are really seen as betrayers of girl power, the liberation of women, and every (so-called) feminist gain.

Now, before I am misunderstood, I will say along with Edith Stein that women are fantastically gifted and able to do nearly everything men can do (save for some obvious physical limitations). But I'm not talking about physical ability; I'm talking about qualities of character that we have been gifted with in a unique way through our feminine nature—particularly women's concern for the vulnerable, our compassion, and what Pope John Paul II called the feminine genius in helping others.

In the Church—as we saw previously with the description of the Marian and Petrine dimensions—we must remember that *both* are necessary, good, fruitful, and beautiful, and all the more so when they work together. No one is served well when the one dimension is privileged over the other. Moreover, no one—not any other organization in the history of the world—has done more to promote the dignity of women than the Catholic Church, even if there have been failings. No other religion has honored women more by emphasizing the importance of monogamy while also exploring the depths of female human nature and dignity. Ironically, since few are aware, this honor bestowed upon women is owed to the distinct person of Our Lady and her role in the gospel and life of the Church. Secular scholar William Lecky emphasized how dramatic Mary's role has been in elevating the status of women: "No longer the slave or toy of man, no longer associated only with ideas of degradation and of sensuality, woman rose, in the person of the Virgin Mother, into a new sphere, and became the object of reverential homage, of which antiquity has no conception . . . A new type of character was called into being; a new kind of admiration was fostered. Into a harsh and ignorant and benighted age, this idea type infused a conception of gentleness and purity, unknown to the proudest civilizations of the past."[1]

Eve was certainly the source of man's disdain for women, but Mary, the New Eve, changed all that. There is no other culture—save those that are living off the fumes of

---

1   William Lecky, *History of Rationalism*, vol. 1 (London: Longmans, Green, and Co., 1866), 234–35.

Christianity—that has upheld the dignity of women in such significant ways.

Role of Motherhood

One of the most important elements of feminine nature that has been allowed to flourish over the centuries through devotion to Mary and the proper understanding of women is the role of motherhood. Motherhood has a unique quality of self-giving built into it. Motherhood has a crash course in growing in virtue embedded into it—*if* we are willing to be transformed—as I've argued in my book *Ultimate Makeover: The Transforming Power of Motherhood*.[2] But there is more to it than that. Women understand (either as biological or as spiritual mothers) that their life has the most meaning when they are living it for someone or something else. While this is not exclusive to women, it is deeply rooted in the female soul.

This general attitude of "my life for yours" is what has animated civilizations from the beginning. We saw this previously in the Gothic period of building in the thirteenth century, when the master builders took on projects that they knew they would never see completed but that would benefit their children and grandchildren. This is the flow that mothers understand. They know they will never see the completion of their own work; a mother never sees the full growth of the seeds she plants, the characters she cultivates, or the souls she helps sanctify, but that doesn't stop her from doing so.

---

2   Carrie Gress, *Ultimate Makeover: The Transforming Power of Motherhood* (Erlanger, KY: Beacon Press, 2016).

This natural flow, however, of one generation to the next not only stopped but started to flow backward in the 1960s. Instead of having children for the sake of those children and their future, children became all about the parents and something they had a right to, or something they had a right *not* to do—first through contraception and then abortion, which the US Supreme Court has told us is necessary because sometimes, contraception fails. Thus the natural flow of civilizations was upended, and this change in flow has had devastating cultural, moral, and psychological effects.

What was "my life for yours" was turned on its head to "your life for mine." This is the true source of what we now know as the "culture of death" that envelops us today. We now see regularly the use of embryonic stem cells and baby body parts (both harvested from aborted babies) as cogs in the supply chain to help the living. Life is changed, cheapened, and chopped up for personal gain, not personal giving.

What is also interesting about our "culture of death" is that like Eve's disobedience, it started with women. The Pill and abortion have largely been choices made by women, with men playing a secondary role. (Of course, there are situations when men and women are forced into contraception/abortion beyond their free will, such as when a woman uses contraception without telling her husband or a woman is forced against her will to abort a child.) Even this anti-Mary movement followed Eve's model of sin.

A quick glance at most any female public figure on the silver screen or in politics only further emphasizes this reverse in the flow. Consider Madonna (whose name is so ironic it would be comical were not it so sad)—the performer and her antics, most of which are too lewd to print—and the politicians that coo about how much they want to help women but have no problem pulling a child apart, limb by limb, in their mother's womb. Most female leaders and supposed role models are at a minimum proabortion and procontraception. These two elements then open the logical threshold of sexual license of every stripe—which has led to a culture that celebrates the vulgar, the brazen and bawdy, the angry and angst-ridden, and the narcissistic. All this is wrapped up neatly in celebrity trimmings, which makes even the vilest characters still appear glamorous, sexy, influential, and rich. It is for this reason that someone like St. Teresa of Kolkata (Mother Teresa) can be reviled by the cultural mavens for the true charity she offered one soul at a time.[3]

Cardinal Mindszenty, who suffered greatly under the Nazis and Communists, presciently said, "For when men no longer understand the infinite charity of God, they will no longer prize the most striking revelation of that charity, the love of mothers."[4] And we are witnessing with front-row

---

3   See Krithika Varagur, "Mother Theresa Was No Saint," *Huffington Post*, March 15, 2016, http://www.huffingtonpost.com/ krithika-varagur/mother-teresa-was-no-saint_b_9470988.html. According to the article, "to canonize Mother Teresa would be to seal the lid on her problematic legacy, which includes forced conversion, questionable relations with dictators, gross mismanagement, and actually, pretty bad medical care. Worst of all, she was the quintessential white person expending her charity on the third world—the entire reason for her public image, and the source of immeasurable scarring to the postcolonial psyche of India and its diaspora."

4   Joseph Mindszenty, *The Face of the Heavenly Mother* (New York: Philosophical Library, 1951), 103.

seats that the reverse of this is also true. When the love of mothers is no longer understood, the infinite charity of God will be forgotten and no longer prized. This can be seen in the children today who have no notion of God yet grasp at any available straw to prove themselves lovable and good. And because they have no one to guide them, they are looking in all the wrong places, and their thirst is never quenched.

It is easy to see, then, that the anti-Mary movement isn't just a possibility; it is already here. But as ever, evil and vice will not have the last word—this should give us a great glimmer of hope.

Mothers: Cultural Cornerstones

Up to now, we have only discussed things that point to an anti-Marian age instead of the Age of Mary. And yet history, popes, the saints, theology, and Our Lady herself suggest the contrary. So what is an Age of Mary? In the past, there were significant indicators that Marian devotion was at the heart of culture. As we have already seen, devotion to Mary not only was evidenced in military conquests and significant evangelization but also spilled over into artwork, innovative architecture, stirring music, and inspired philosophy. These are decidedly not the markers of our current culture.

In order to determine why all this bad news might in fact be good news, it's important to look at the significant shifts that have renewed the Church over the years. There is a pattern that can be traced through many struggles in the Church. In the thirteenth century, the Church was choking on its wealth. Among the many saints of that era, who was sent? The *poverello*, the "poor man," St. Francis. And as we have seen, when the world was filled with pagan symbolism, St. Benedict fled the city and reseeded civilization free from pagan weeds. The saints of an age (the creative minorities) serve as hints to what is most in need of change in the broader culture. We have ample suggestions of what needs to be changed today—namely, narcissism, celebrity adulation, and deep sexual sin. Small hints are cropping up to indicate how God, through His saints, will transform these vices.

Pope John Paul II's theology of the body is one such example offered as an antidote to rampant sexual sin. Another example of God working in a purposeful way is seen in the saintly soul of Father Flanagan. Among his many gifts and his intense devotion to Mary, he was profoundly attached to the idea of the "anawim," or the small ones of God, and trying to imitate the best model of humility—Mary. Even as the founder of an order, it was not uncommon to find him sleeping in a chair because he had given his bed to a new novice for the night. Moreover, in this emphasis on the small, he avoided any sort of limelight (which is why most people have never heard of him). He turned down *TIME*'s request for a feature article on his order and decades of other media requests. Although he was handsome, a war hero, a two-time national football champion at Notre Dame, and the son of a prominent judge, he remained simply an unknown and humble priest from Boston who reached out to the poor around the world in dramatic ways. He was modeling the "anticelebrity" in an age when celebrity is king and notions of smallness and obedience are mocked.

The saints of an age, like Father Flanagan, are those who live most contrary to the spirit of the age.

Motherhood also offers a profound example of the kind of sanctity needed today. Mothers are the cornerstones of culture. Living motherhood with quiet humility couldn't be further from the current ethos, but like previous ages, what is so attacked is precisely the antidote that is needed. Satan has tempted women in every conceivable way to reject motherhood as a value. As a result, more than fifty-five million children in the United States alone have been destroyed through abortion, and millions of women suffer in silence because of their lost motherhood. In New York City alone, the statistics are staggering: for every 1,000 live births, there are 598 abortions.[5]

By trying to see what is happening to our culture, we can see what Satan is trying to do and what he's trying to destroy. He goes after the greatest good. Motherhood is one of the greatest goods of any society because of the transformation women can have in men and in raising children. If man is unable to find an earthly icon of femininity, then not only is it impossible to convey what a proper mother is, what she does, and how vital she is, but our links to the perfect maternity of Mary are severed, leaving humanity bereft of the concept of motherhood entirely. "It is through the mediation of women," a theologian has noted, "that men are increasingly

---

5   Center for Disease Control, "Morbidity and Mortality Weekly Report: Abortion Surveillance—United States, 2013," November 25, 2016, https://www.cdc.gov/mmwr/volumes/65/ss/ss6512a1.htm.

given anew to society."[6] Without women's good influence, society cannot renew itself.

Despite all this pressure on women and the depth of the sins against the family in particular, Mary has not remained dormant or inactive. Not only is she here to assist us; she is the antidote to these cultural issues. French priest Father André Feuillet, who experienced the painful edges of the twentieth century, wrote in 1974, "The Christian Church is presently experiencing a very severe crisis. The most evangelical way of viewing this, without in any way trying to minimize it and without ceasing to call evil what is so in fact, is to see in this terrible trial the *painful childbearing of a new Christian world.* Just like the time of the Passion of Christ, these times we live in are very especially the *Hour of the Woman* above all, therefore, the Hour of the Woman par excellence of the new covenant, the Hour of Mary."[7]

While Father Feuillet was referring to the Church in the immediate aftermath of the Second Vatican Council, his remarks extend well beyond the 1970s and can be applied to today. As we have seen, Satan is trying to undercut women and undercut the Woman from Scripture with whom he remains in battle.

Feuillet compares the trials of our age to birth pangs. Like the struggle, labor, pain, and sorrow involved with childbirth, all these will give way when something new is ushered in by Our Mother.

---

6   André Feuillet, *Jesus and His Mother* (Petersham, MA: St. Bede's Publication, 1984), 206–7.

7   Ibid., 239.

The Age of Mary

Beyond the evidence that women and the Woman are being taken out at the knees by Satan, there are other signs of a rising Marian Age. Mariologist Father Roten has described what some pieces of a Marian Age look like. Among them are (1) a rediscovery of religion in general, (2) the search for a more personal and relational expression of devotion, (3) the rediscovery of popular religion as an antidote to secularization, (4) the multiplication of apparitions, and (5) the rediscovery of devotions and spiritual movements.[8] Certainly, these five elements are on the rise in pockets of the world, if not on a massive scale. Many young people who were largely unchurched are discovering the Catholic faith, particularly as they reject the culture of death. Other people who have faith already are looking to go deeper, trying to find new ways to draw closer to God.

As for apparitions, the "Miracle Hunter" Michael O'Neill said that in recent decades, there have been roughly two thousand five hundred reported apparitions of Mary. We are also seeing continued development in Mariology and the swelling of popular devotions to Mary.

Father Roten has noted that there are distinct characteristics to the current trends toward Marian devotion. First, these devotions have a strong *iconic* character, meaning that icons, medals, and scapulars with the Marian image create a visual connection. The fact that the visual is so popular

---

8   Johann G. Roten, "The Age of Mary," *International Marian Research Institute*, https://www.udayton.edu/imri/mary/a/age-of-mary.php.

shouldn't surprise us when we look at a culture saturated by images. This is, at least, a positive use of visual imagery.

Second, there is "a *narrative* dimension" that places Mary in a biblical context, such as in the Rosary or the angelus or through pilgrimages to Marian shrines. And third, there is "a *mystagogical* development, meaning the growing importance of entrusting to Mary in acts of consecration in order for her to lead us closer to Jesus (Eucharist) or to associate us to her own mission."[9] Mystagogy is a fancy way of saying that Mary leads us to her Son—that she helps facilitate deeper meetings and connections between her spiritual children and their Savior. Entrusting ourselves to her opens the door farther to allow her to work more deeply in our lives.

Contemporary Popes and Mary

Among the popes, there has been a significant increase in writings about Mary in the last two centuries. The time period from 1850 to 1950 is often called the "the Marian Century" because of the pronouncements of the two Marian dogmas: the Immaculate Conception in 1854 and Mary's Assumption into heaven in 1950, by Popes Pius IX and Pius XII, respectively. Pope Leo XIII wrote twelve encyclicals about Mary and the Rosary in the late 1800s and early 1900s. In the Second Vatican Council documents—particularly *Lumen Gentium*—the teachings about Mary outweighed all the council teachings about Mary up to that point. Pope Paul VI also wrote extensively about Mary, followed by Pope John Paul II, who has been called "the pope of the

---

9   Ibid.

Rosary." Pope Benedict XVI and Pope Francis have made explicit their devotion to the Rosary and Our Lady, while Pope Francis has popularized devotion to Our Lady Undoer of Knots.

Her Immaculate Triumph

There has been much speculation about what is happening in our world. Mary's words at Fatima have added another layer of mystery to the confusing landscape. On June 13, 1917, Mary told the three children at Fatima that, despite wars, the spread of Russia's errors, and the suffering of the pope, "in the end, my Immaculate Heart will Triumph." Many have speculated on her precise meaning.[10] What is clear, however, is that Mary's role is not yet finished. As St. Louis de Montfort explained, "It was through Mary that Jesus Christ came into the world, and it is also through her that he must reign in the world."[11] And "this maternity of Mary in the order of grace . . . will last without interruption until the eternal fulfillment of all the elect"[12]—that is, Mary's work will continue until she brings home all of her children.

We can rest assured that despite the weakness of our culture, and no matter how malicious and vile Satan's attacks

---

10 "Revelations of the Immaculate Heart at Fatima in 1917," *EWTN*, https://www.ewtn.com/library/MARY/FIRSTSAT .HTM.

11 St. Louis de Montfort, *True Devotion to Mary* (Charlotte, NC: TAN Books, 2010), 1; cf. 13, 22, 49, 157, 217, 262.

12 Pope John Paul II, *Redemptoris Mater*, March 25, 1987, #22, *The Holy See*, http://w2.vatican.va/content/john-paul-ii/en/ encyclicals/documents/hf_jp-ii_enc_25031987_redemptoris -mater.html#%241A.

are, his power is far surpassed by the power of the Virgin Mary. Mary will always be stronger. Why? Because she is the power of love, not hate, pride, ego, and envy.

Yes, we live in a troubling time, and yes, there are those who have abandoned God, but God and His mother never abandon us. We know through Mary's perseverance at Calvary at the foot of Christ's Cross that she remains here with us in the thick of the battle. She will not leave us orphans.

Father Amorth, the late Vatican exorcist, reminds us that "the tribulations of the Church will have an end. And the finale will be good: God will have the last word on history."[13] Although quite different than previous Marian moments, we have the reassurance that she is here for us and preparing for the triumph of her Immaculate Heart. What exactly that means remains to be seen, but we know it will be good.

---

13   Gabriele Amorth, *An Exorcist Explains the Demonic* (Manchester, NH: Sophia Press, 2016), 122.

PART IV

Living the Marian Option

CHAPTER 11

The Simple Remedy

When the atomic bomb was dropped on Hiroshima on August 6, 1945, the large Japanese city was flattened. Within seconds, half a million people were gone—vaporized by the blast. A charred, smoldering swathe remained where a once thriving city stood. Miraculously, one mile from the detonation point, one structure, though badly damaged, remained in the sea of nothing—the Jesuit church of Our Lady of the Assumption. Not only did the church survive the blast, but four Jesuit priests came through the cataclysmic event with nothing but a few scratches, and none experienced deadly radiation side effects. Father Schiffer, one of the surviving priests, said they attributed their survival to the Blessed Virgin Mary: "We were living the message of Fatima. We lived and prayed the rosary daily."[1]

---

1   "Hubert Schiffer," *Wikipedia*, last modified January 9, 2017, https://en.wikipedia.org/wiki/Hubert_Schiffer.

When feeling pressure from outside world, our first impulse is to think of something huge to transform the world. When "the huge" eludes us, we are left feeling helpless and ineffective. But the Marian Option asks for the small, the hidden—tiny acts performed, as Mother Teresa said, with great love. St. Thérèse of the Child Jesus in her "little way" exemplified this, which made her a doctor of the Church. Like Naaman the leper in Scripture, who was told by the prophet Eliseus to simply wash seven times in the river and went away angry because the cure was so simple, often Christians look past the Rosary because it isn't complicated or grand enough (2 Kgs 5).

While there are other elements of the Marian Option that can be included, such as Marian Consecration and the Angelus (see also the appendix), the Rosary is at the heart of devotion to Our Lady. There is a reason the Rosary has been called the spiritual weapon of our times by St. (Padre) Pio and others: it has proven to be effective time after time.[2] Like the tiny stone thrown by David to vanquish Goliath, the small beads of the rosary can rid the world of the evils represented by the Philistine, such as pride, impurity, and heresy. Only the humble (the anawim) can access this spring of power, while the prideful are confounded by its littleness.

---

2   Sam Guzman, "A Powerful Weapon: 15 Quotes on the Holy Rosary," *Catholic Gentleman* (blog), October 7, 2014, http://www.catholic gentleman.net/2014/10/powerful-weapon-15-quotes-holy-rosary. For more on this, see Donald Calloway, *Champions of the Rosary* (Stockbridge, MA: Marian Press, 2016).

History of the Rosary

At first glance, the rosary seems a simple enough thing: beads mark off Our Father and Hail Mary prayers, with each set of ten representing a different mystery of Christ and Mary's life. How this understanding of the rosary came to us is a much longer and fascinating story.

The origins of the rosary go back to at least the fourth century and the desert fathers. Paul of Thebes (234–347 A.D.), an Egyptian hermit, used three hundred small pebbles to keep track of his penitential prayers, while St. Anthony (251–356 A.D.) used knotted string to keep track of prayers in the desert of Syria. Eventually, the notion of stringing the pebbles together arose, making the work of counting much less work.

The prayer that was counted on the beads most often was the Our Father—the *Paternoster* in Latin—until around the twelfth century. One hundred and fifty beads were strung together so Paternosters could be prayed by the illiterate, who made up the majority of the population (including many religious). This served as a replacement for the Liturgy of the Hours, which required the ability to read the psalms in Latin. Eventually, the practice became so popular among the faithful that crafters of the beads acquired their own street in London, named Paternoster Row, where four guilds of artisans worked to create the linked beads.

The Paternoster beads eventually began to include Ave Marias, particularly as the rich Mariology being written by such men as St. Bernard of Clairvaux spread beyond the cloister walls. Monks and laity alike wanted to find new ways to express their devotion to the Lady, Full of Grace, and so a Marian psalter, similar to the Liturgy of the Hours, was developed, containing one hundred fifty prayers prayed on beads. Eventually, one Our Father was added to every set of ten Hail Marys, making fifteen decades for the psalter.

Then in the early thirteenth century, St. Dominic and his followers, the Dominicans, were in a fierce theological fight against the Albigensian heresy. Unable to rid Southern France of this intellectual plague, St. Dominic resorted to intense prayer and fasting. Shortly thereafter, Our Lady visited him and told him that the key to conquering the Albigensian heresy was to pray the Marian psalter. Taking his Mother's advice, St. Dominic not only prayed but preached the Marian psalter far and wide, and the Albigensian heresy quickly vanished. The efficacy behind the psalter has been viewed symbolically as offering Mary a rose with each prayer, which is eventually how the faithful arrived at the name "rosary."

The Marian psalter was said to wane in popularity during the thirteenth century because of the tumult of the Black Death and then experienced a resurgence because of the work of Blessed Alan de la Roche (1428–75) in the fifteenth century. Blessed Alan finally formalized the name of the Rosary (replacing the more common name of Marian psalter), promoted confraternities, and urged priests to preach the Rosary to transform their parishes while encouraging families to pray it to transform their homes.

One curious element is that in times of struggle, devotion to the Rosary often increases, but that was not the case in the thirteenth century during the Black Death. What did increase was devotion to the Angelus prayer—clearly people were calling upon their spiritual Mother, just not as frequently through the Rosary.[3]

But in returning to these two surges in popularity of the Rosary—St. Dominic's and then Blessed Alan de la Roche's—we might be struck by the fact that they preceded two major events that rocked the Church and the European world. In St. Dominic's time, it was certainly the Albigensians but also a massive series of plagues and warfare, making the thirteenth century second only to the twentieth century in violence, massive loss of life, and major societal upheaval. The dreadful events of the thirteenth century spawned significant speculation that the apocalypse was near. Later, when Blessed Alan was guided by Our Lady through interior promptings to again promote the Rosary, what followed was the Protestant Reformation, which sent Europe reeling from wars, persecutions, and societal crumbling by those "protesting" the Church. The Rosary was Our Lady's way of preparing the people for these most difficult times.

The Eastern Orthodox Church also has something akin to the Rosary, known as the Rule of the Mother of God. It too was said to have been given by Our Lady herself around the eighth century, although to whom is unknown. Although the Eastern version of the Hail Mary is slightly different,

---

3   The second half of the Hail Mary, "Holy Mary, Mother of God, pray for us sinners now and at the hour of our death," was added during the plagues because so many were so near death in the wake of the disease.

it is also prayed on one hundred fifty beads.[4] St. Seraphim
Zvezdinsky of Sarov (1754–1833) is generally credited with
popularizing the rule in the eighteenth century. A letter
of one of his disciples comes down to us, so we have a sense of
how it was promoted during St. Seraphim's time:

> I forgot to give you a piece of advice vital for salva-
> tion. Say the "O Hail, Mother of God and Virgin"
> one hundred and fifty times, and this prayer will
> lead you on the way to salvation. This rule was given
> by the Mother of God herself in about the eighth
> century . . . In my hands I have a hand-written book
> from the cell of St. Seraphim, containing a description
> of the many miracles which took place through pray-
> ing to the Mother of God and especially through say-
> ing one hundred and fifty times (15 decades) the "O
> Hail, Mother of God." If, being unaccustomed to it, it
> is difficult to master one hundred and fifty repetitions
> daily, say it fifty times at first (5 decades).[5]

All this overlaps remarkably with what the saints in the
Roman Church had been saying for centuries and very closely
resembles the popular devotion to the Rosary in the West.

One of the unsung benefits of the Rosary and the rule is
that is has helped the illiterate or those who had not been

---

4   The Eastern version of the Hail Mary is as follows: "Rejoice, O
    Mother of God and Virgin, Mary full of Grace, the Lord is with
    thee. Blessed art thou among women and blessed is the fruit of
    thy womb, for thou has brought forth the Savior of our souls."

5   Christopher Warner, *Rule of the Mother of God: The Eastern Rosa-
    ry of Saint Seraphim* (2009), 5.

catechized in the Faith understand the central mysteries of the Faith. This had the added benefit of eliminating minor heresies or misunderstandings that arose from folk beliefs (the major heresies always started with clergy).[6] The Rosary, then, as a devotion, helps keep heresy at bay. This is not surprising, given that Mary is known as Destroyer of Heresies. "The great power of the Rosary," Blessed Cardinal John Henry Newman said, "consists in the fact that it translates the Creed into Prayer. Of course, the Creed is already in a certain sense a prayer and a great act of homage towards God, but the Rosary brings us to meditate again on the great truth of His life and death, and brings this truth close to our hearts."[7] The meditations on Christ's life—even in their various forms—taught the illiterate much about the Faith while weeding out false teachings.

Rosary Through the Ages

While devotion to the Rosary has waned and waxed, there has been a consistent call for it both by the saints and by Our Lady herself during the apparitions that have full Church approval, particularly Lourdes and Fatima. Our Lady said to Blessed Alan de la Roche that "after the Holy Sacrifice of the Mass, which is the most important as well as the Living Memorial of Our Blessed Lord's Passion, there could not be a finer devotion or one of greater merit than that of the

---

6   Anne Winston-Allen, *Stories of the Rose* (University Park, PA: Penn State University Press, 1997), 28.

7   Quoted from "Why Pray the Rosary Every Day for a Year?," *365 Rosaries*, http://365rosaries.blogspot.com/2010/06/june-22-saints-thomas-more-and-john.html.

Rosary."[8] Blessed Pope Pius XI maintained, "The Rosary is a powerful weapon to put the demons to flight and to keep oneself from sin. If you desire peace in your hearts, in your homes, and in your country, assemble each evening to recite the Rosary. Let not even one day pass without saying it, no matter how burdened you may be with many cares and labors."[9] St. Josemaría Escrivá, founder of Opus Dei, said, "The holy Rosary is a powerful weapon. Use it with confidence and you'll be amazed at the results."[10]

Among the many fruits of the Rosary, the Virgin Mary spoke to Blessed Alan about what a community that prays the Rosary looks like:

> Through the rosary, hardened sinners of both sexes became converted and started to lead a holy life, bemoaning their past sins with genuine tears of contrition. Even children performed unbelievable penances: devotion to my Son and to me spread so thoroughly that it almost seemed as though angels were living on earth. The Faith was gaining, and many Catholics longed to shed their blood for it and fight against the heretics. Thus, through the sermons of my very dear Dominic and through the power of the rosary, the heretics' lands were all brought under the Church.

---

8   St. Louis de Montfort, "Twenty-Eighth Rose: Salutary Effects," in *The Secret of the Rosary* (New York: Montfort Publications, 1954), http://www.catholictradition.org/Classics/secret-rosary28.htm.

9   Guzman, "Powerful Weapon."

10   Ibid.

People used to give munificent alms; hospitals and churches were built. People led moral and law-abiding lives and worked wonders for the glory of God. Holiness and unworldliness flourished; the clergy were exemplary, princes were just, people lived at peace with each other and justice and equity reigned in the guilds and in the homes.

I must not fail to mention the signs and wonders that I have wrought in different lands through the holy rosary: I have stopped pestilences and put an end to horrible wars as well as to bloody crimes, and through the rosary people have found the courage to flee temptation.[11]

Perhaps this all sounds a bit too good to be true, but then, looking back at Marian intercession, much of it is just that—too good to be true. And yet, that is what we should expect from the Mother of Mercy.

How the Rosary "Works"

Much of the Rosary's popularity rests upon its simplicity, but once again, that simplicity does not translate into the superficial. "The rosary has been extolled as a 'compendium of the entire Gospel' and a meditation on the mysteries of the Lord's life and salvific work seen through the eyes of his mother," Mariologist Father Johann Roten has explained. "It

---

11   As quoted in de Montfort, *Secret of the Rosary*, 119; Our Lady's Word to Blessed Alan de la Roche in Calloway, *Champions of the Rosary*, Appendix B.

is as if Mary were the narrator of the events mentioned, a narrator who was part of the story and still holds an active role in the ongoing event of salvation."[12]

While there are many unknowns about the efficacy of the Rosary and the impression it makes on heaven, Father Roten has explained how it makes an impression on us by comparing it to pilgrimages. Pilgrimages are one of the oldest forms of worship found in every major religion. Part of the draw is to leave our everyday lives (the profane) and seek out the sacred in places like St. Peter's Basilica, Santiago de Compostela, or Marian shrines. (Pope John Paul used to call these the places where you could hear the mother's "heartbeat.")

Once we arrive at the sacred, we enter into something beyond us—something that we know will transform us. We enter into the memory of the Christian story, but sometimes we find new graces, new insights, or even healing that change us. Few people leave a pilgrimage site without feeling transformed in some way. As we return to the everyday, we bring with us something of the sacred and pass it along—even in the smallest of ways—to those around us.

In order to embark on a pilgrimage, we don't necessarily have to go very far. Attending Mass has similar effects of seeking out the sacred, experiencing the divine, and entering back into the world. Even visiting a local church and praying in front of the tabernacle, a beautiful icon, or a statue can imitate the effect of a pilgrimage.

---

12   Johann G. Roten, "Marian Devotion for the New Millennium," *Marian Studies* 51 (2000), 84, http://ecommons.udayton.edu/marian_studies/vol51/iss1/7.

The Rosary can transform us in a similar way. By setting aside time to pray it, we mentally leave the everyday, going from the profane in search of the sacred. By focusing on the mysteries of Christ's life, we remember the Christian story. In that encounter, we are transformed through new graces, insights, or healing. At the end of the Rosary, we have been transformed—even if just in the slightest way—which then allows us to reenter the world to share what we have been given.

In chapter 1, we saw how a mystic can transform the world as a creative minority. Historian Arnold Toynbee's exhaustive work reveals that mystics can leave the world through prayer and come back to transform it, often in incredible ways. This is precisely the same process we see in this idea of pilgrimage, even if it is just the short journey through the mysteries of the Rosary.

St. Louis de Montfort offered a different explanation for the Rosary's efficacy—that of imitation. "Children copy their parents through watching them and talking to them," the French saint explained, "and they learn their own language through hearing them speak. An apprentice learns his trade through watching his master at work; in the same way . . . the Holy Rosary can become like their divine Master if they reverently study and imitate the virtues of Jesus which are shown in the fifteen mysteries of his life."[13] By meditating on Christ's virtues, Our Lady helps instruct us in those same patterns as we work out our salvation.

---

13   de Montfort, *Secrets of the Rosary*, 186.

One of the most remarkable elements of Marian devotion is that it transforms us—but not into someone that has
already existed, like a carbon copy of saints of old; rather,
it "seeks to nourish the image of God in each person and
to promote our God-likeness as individuals in the Communion of Saints."[14] It calls individuals "to become who God
already knows them to be—to become who they already
are."[15] There is nothing cookie-cutter about holiness; instead,
it makes us more unique the deeper we dive into it.

Consecration to Our Lady

St. Louis de Montfort has offered Christians a deeper way to
devote ourselves to Mary: the Marian consecration. He calls
it the "easiest way to get to heaven." By making ourselves her
"slaves," we offer up and give to her everything that belongs
to us—including even the rewards of any good actions—and
she in turn transforms them into something better than we
could have imagined. Like the peasants of old who knew
that they could get to the king through the kind heart of
the queen, Marian consecration offers Mary our littleness,
which through her greatness and love, is transformed into
something beautiful for God.

Marian consecration, then, takes devotion to another
level—the highest level. As Father Roten has explained, when
a person is consecrated to Jesus through Mary, "the existential
bond with Jesus through Mary is here not only symbolized
through a medal or scapular, it also becomes an existential and

---

14   Roten, "Marian Devotion," 86.
15   Ibid.

embodied reality and dedication of the whole person."[16] Pope St. John Paul II attested to this when he said, "In repeating every day 'Totus tuus [totally yours],' and living in harmony with her, one can attain to the experience of the Father in limitless confidence and love, to docility to the Holy Spirit, and to the transformation of self according to the image of Christ."[17]

Consecration to Mary unites us to her and the Holy Trinity in a very unique way because of the relationships she shares with all of them.

When Evil Increases

One of the most common struggles today is feeling as if our prayers aren't really doing anything in the face of such expansive evil. The reality is that we should not despair but remember first that the world doesn't need huge numbers to transform it. Perhaps more important, we should remember the spiritual weapons we have at our disposal and not underestimate them. There is a well-known quote often attributed to St. Ignatius: "Work as if everything depended on you; trust as if everything depended on God." We would do well to remember this sage advice. Pope Paul VI also reminds us that "if evils increase, the devotion of the People of God should also increase."[18] And finally, Pope John Paul II offers

---

16   Ibid.
17   "His Holiness Pope John Paul II Reveals Virgin Mary Role in His Life," *ZENIT*, October 15, 2000, http://www.zeitun-eg.org/jp2.htm.
18   Pope Paul VI, *Christi Matri*, September 15, 1966, #9, *The Holy See*, http://w2.vatican.va/content/paul-vi/en/encyclicals/documents/hf_p-vi_enc_15091966_christi-matri.html.

us confidence that we can find much hope in the Rosary: "The history of the rosary shows how this prayer was used in particular by the Dominicans at a difficult time for the Church due to the spread of heresy." The Polish pope continues, "Today we are facing new challenges. Why should we not once more have recourse to the rosary, with the same faith as those who have gone before us?"[19] But perhaps the best description of the Rosary's power was given by Blessed Pope Pius IX (1792–1878): "Give me an army saying the Rosary and I will conquer the world."[20]

Those to Whom Much Has Been Given

There is a story that tells of a priest, doing missionary work in Japan, attending an international event that brought together Christians from around the world as well as foreign dignitaries. The Japanese ambassador approached the priest and said, "War is your fault." Surprised by such a stark statement, the priest asked what he meant. The ambassador answered, "You Catholics, all of you—we do not have peace in the world. It is your fault."

The priest asked for more clarification. "Ambassador, why do you blame us?"

"I've read about this," he replied. "The Lady came to you at Fatima, right? That's what you believe? She told you what

---

19   Pope John Paul II, *Rosarium Virginis Mariae*, October 16, 2002, #17, *The Holy See*, https://w2.vatican.va/content/john-paul-ii/en/apost_letters/2002/documents/hf_jp-ii_apl_20021016_rosarium-virginis-mariae.html.

20   Guzman, "Powerful Weapon."

to do to secure peace in the world. Well, there's no peace in the world, so obviously you Catholics haven't done it."

The priest, acknowledging that the ambassador was right, still protested, "Isn't peace everyone's responsibility?"

The ambassador spoke vehemently, "No, she came to you Catholics. Not to Buddhists. Not to Hindus. She came to you, and it is your responsibility."[21]

While it is hard to ascertain if this conversation really happened, what we do know is that the ambassador was right: Mary did come to Catholics. She has told us how to bring peace to the world, and we have a responsibility to do it not just for ourselves or our children but for the whole world.

Like other Christs, we are called to make sacrifices and step into the gap of what is lacking in others to help bring salvation to those who don't know how to acquire it themselves. As the Good Book says, "To those who have been given much, much is expected. And unto whomsoever much is given, of him much shall be required: and to whom they have committed much, of him they will demand the more" (Lk 12:48).

Often we get caught up in our daily lives, and it is easy to forget all the incredible things that Mary has done and is doing in the world. It is easy to forget the simple solutions available to us and the world through her powerful intercession. We can also forget that what we have been entrusted

---

21   Donald Calloway, "Five First Saturdays in Reparation to the Immaculate Heart of Mary," *Thirteenth of the Month Club*, http://www.marian.org/13th/firstsaturday.php.

with is both a privilege and a responsibility—something we
will be held accountable for when we face God's judgment.

But when we do get caught up in the things of this world,
the solution doesn't need to be overwhelming. In fact, it's
very simple: grab your rosary and turn to Our Lady. Servant
of God Sister Lúcia de Santos, one of the children of Fatima,
has assured us that "the Most Holy Virgin in these last times
in which we live has given a new efficacy to the recitation
of the Rosary to such an extent that there is no problem,
no matter how difficult it is, whether temporal or above
all spiritual, in the personal life of each one of us, of our
families . . . that cannot be solved by the Rosary." The Por-
tuguese nun emphasized, "There is no problem, I tell you,
no matter how difficult it is, that we cannot resolve by the
prayer of the Holy Rosary."[22]

---

22   Calloway, *Champions of the Rosary*, 247.

CHAPTER 12

Mary Prepares Us for Anything

We live in dark times, and our media-driven culture has made us more aware of the struggles our culture has before us. The news cycle contributes to an increase in general chaos, violence, and uneasiness instead of peace, solace, and hope.

When faced with violence, disease, and natural disasters, there's an impulse in all of us to want to run and hide. This impulse dates back to the early Church and the apostles, as when St. Peter left Rome to escape being crucified. Our Lord met him on the way and asked him the famous question, *Quo vadis?* ("Where are you going?"). Truly, it was Our Lord's will that Peter follow Him in the ultimate sacrifice. Of late, the "rapture movement" among Protestants has earned millions in book sales and films from those looking for some assurance that they won't have to suffer what other Christians have suffered throughout the ages.

Fear, human weakness, vulnerability, brokenness, and sin can all add weight to the burden of difficult times. It's natural to want to turn away from the difficulties—from the

Cross—but Christians are called to not live naturally but supernaturally, to live with God's grace. But to live with this grace, we must not merely rely on what is natural. We must seek out sources of grace.

As we have seen, Mary is a tremendous source of grace. As our Mother, she will help prepare us to endure whatever might come our way. Not only will she not leave us orphans; she will help raise us to be spiritual adults. Popes, saints, and the witness of those who love Mary reveal that her maternal care extends to the cultivation of our own souls. Mary, the secret gardener—or "the heavenly gardener," as she was called by St. Thérèse of Lisieux—helps her children become better followers of her Son by facilitating the maturation of their souls. John Paul II explained, "For, 'with maternal love she cooperates in the birth and development' of the sons and daughters of Mother Church."[1] As a person under her care matures, he or she becomes more and more capable to take on whatever the world (and the Devil) throws at him or her.

Spiritual adulthood is rarely discussed in our culture or in the Church. Sadly, most people in the pews today had their catechetical formation halted at about the eighth-grade level. They received confirmation, but it was treated as an end of the journey instead of just a beginning. Of course, this is a reflection of the times in which we live more than upon any single individual.

---

1   Pope John Paul II, *Redemptoris Mater*, March 25, 1987, #44, *The Holy See*, http://w2.vatican.va/content/john-paul-ii/en/ encyclicals/documents/hf_jp-ii_enc_25031987_redemptoris -mater.html#%241A.

In 1906, sociologist Arnold van Gennep explained that cultures require a certain type of regeneration in order to sustain themselves; the culture will fall to pieces without new lifeblood. This lifeblood comes, van Gennep argued, by having one generation raise the next generation into spiritual adulthood. Few parents think of the essential reality of bringing their children to spiritual adulthood. Confirmation, as they experienced it, seems to be the capstone; after that, it's up to the child. But being children, other interests—largely material—eclipse the spiritual, so typically, the full spiritual maturation of the soul doesn't happen until much later in life, if at all. We have sufficient evidence of elderly individuals who are still not spiritually mature.

This spiritual immaturity is something Our Mother eradicates. Even the children to whom she has appeared, though tender of age, showed incredible signs of spiritual maturity. Jacinta at Fatima, Lúcia later told us, was incredibly mature and wise beyond her years before her death at the age of ten.

Spiritual maturity is also a crucial piece of a creative minority. If you don't have individuals who know how to pray and truly connect with God, then you cannot have what Arnold Toynbee called "the mystic," or those who pray and then return to the world with a plan of action and regeneration. Without spiritual maturity, you can't get people like St. Benedict, St. Gregory the Great, or St. Dominic. The culture is left in the hands of spiritual children—the spiritually childish.

The richest irony in all of this is that we are encouraged to become like children in that children trust easily, obey beloved parents, and listen intently to the voice of the Father.

As for our Mother, we depend on her "for the maintenance and increase of our spiritual life as Christ depended on her for the maintenance and increase of his corporal life."[2] She is the one who will bring us to full maturity, particularly those who have consecrated themselves to her. The world might tell us to be self-reliant, but the truly wise are dependent on her and have confidence in her maternal care. St. Thérèse, along with her namesake, St. Teresa of Ávila, are just two of many saints who lost a mother early, only to ask Our Lady to take their earthy mother's place. At age five, St. Thérèse "pronounced the Act of Consecration to the Blessed Virgin." Years later, she explained, "In consecrating myself to the Virgin Mary, I asked her to watch over me, placing into the act all the devotion of my soul, and it seemed to me, I saw her once again looking down and smiling on her 'petite fleur.'"[3]

St. Catherine Labouré, on the day of her mother's death when she was just nine years old, climbed up on a chair and took a statue of Our Lady off a shelf in her parents' room. Addressing it with childlike fervor, she said, "Now, dear Blessed Mother, now you will be my Mother!"[4] She

2   "William Joseph Chaminade in Vignettes and Cameos," *International Marian Research Institute*, https://www.udayton.edu/imri/mary/w/william-joseph-chaminade-in-vignettes-and-cameos.php#anchor6.

3   From Thérèse of Lisieux, *Story of a Soul* (Washington, DC: ICS Publications, 1996), qtd. by John Hardon, "Devotion of St. Thérèse of Lisieux to the Blessed Virgin Mary," *Review for Religious* 11 (March 1952): 75–84, http://www.therealpresence.org/archives/Saints/Saints_027.htm.

4   Joseph Dirvin, *Saint Catherine Labouré of the Miraculous Medal* (Charlotte, NC: TAN Books, 1984), http://www.ewtn.com/library/MARY/CATLABOU.HTM.

then put the statue back on the shelf and left. Clearly, her request was heard. The apparition she had of Our Lady is said to be one of the most intimate because she was able to speak to her directly for hours, like a true daughter to her mother. St. Catherine recalled even the sound her silk dress made whenever she arrived.

We know that Mary does not offer us something naïve or overly sugarcoated about Christian trials. She told both St. Bernadette at Lourdes and the three children at Fatima that they would suffer much: "I cannot promise you happiness on earth, but I can promise you happiness in heaven." And yet all of them were very willing to suffer for her, for her Son, and for the conversion of sinners. But like she has told so many of the saints, there is nothing to fear.

Part of the maturation process includes coming to find joy and consolation in the Cross instead of just pain. St. Maximilian Kolbe explains further, "Give everything over to her will—whether she wants to give us sweets or nourish us with dryness; be close to her by your will, in her arms. Her way of the Immaculate, even though it be strewn at times with crosses and suffering, is not, nevertheless, all that burdensome and obscure."[5] Mary helps her children see the Cross in light of love—the way her Son did as a gift of self for others. Mary always takes us to the Cross, reminding us of the depth of her Son's love for each of us.

For some of us, our biggest obstacle to Christ is embracing our own cross. Often, we wish it away or wish that we

---

5   Maximilian Kolbe, *Let Yourself Be Led by the Immaculate* (Kansas City: Angelus Press, 2013), Kindle ed., loc. 382.

had a different one. Yet our crosses contribute much not just to our life as individuals but to the world beyond us. Stanisław Grygiel, who was a close friend of Pope John Paul II, explains:

> Without the *scientia cruces* [the science of the cross] of people who stand under the cross, society becomes a mass of individuals who may at times function intelligently, but who always act stupidly, because they lack the meaning to which the empty tomb points. They debase themselves in their hiding places, where they seek a refuge that allows them to escape the cross. This anthropological error, which consists in refusing to be *martyrion*, makes them fall prey to the conviction that life is exhausted here and now, *in saeculo* [in time]. Hiding, this is, fleeing from the cross and the empty tomb, they become secularized.[6]

In effect, Grygiel says, every time we reject the Cross, we are seeking refuge in something else. Everything that takes away from the Cross is merely a distraction from what is truly real—from what is the source of our existence and the source of order, meaning, and love. In this short insight, Grygiel offers a keen look at how secularization happens. Rather than being a symbol of progress or perfection, it is a turning away from the Cross, trying to whitewash earthly life of what makes demands on us. It is the desire to remain a spiritual child.

---

6   Stanisław Grygiel, *Discovering the Human Person* (Grand Rapids, MI: Eerdmans, 2014), 87.

Mary assists in transforming civilization and rolling back secularization one soul at a time. As Father Paul Scalia has pointed out, "devotion to her brings purity to the soul and therefore clarity to the mind."[7] We certainly have evidence of this in the medieval scholastics who were keenly devoted to her and reached intellectual heights that have scarcely been reached again.[8] But her influence extends to all her children, not just the philosophers and theologians. The Beatitudes speak of the blessedness of "the pure of heart, for they shall see God" (Mt 5:8). Mary helps purify our hearts, which results in seeing God. It is in seeing and knowing God that we are inoculated from wanting to hide from the Cross.

Archbishop Fulton Sheen speaks of the unique role women have within civilization, and Mary is no different: "A mother is outside time. She dies, but she is still a mother. She is the image of the eternal in time, the shadow of the infinite on the finite. Centuries and civilizations dissolve, but the mother is the giver of life. Man works on his generation; a mother on the next. A man uses life; a mother renews it."[9] Not only does a mother renew life by giving life to the next generation; she plants the seeds that flourish into culture. Archbishop Sheen adds, "Culture derives from woman—for had she not taught her children to talk, the

---

7   Paul Scalia, "Mary, Destroyer of All Heresies," *The Catholic Thing*, August 4, 2016, https://www.thecatholicthing.org/ 2016/08/14/mary-destroyer-of-all-heresies.

8   Their achievements should not be confused with scientific progress, which is quite different.

9   Fulton J. Sheen, *The World's First Love*, 2nd ed. (San Francisco: Ignatius Press, 2010), 188.

great spiritual values of the world would not have passed from generation to generation. After nourishing the substance of the body to which she gave birth, she then nourishes the child with the substance of her mind. As guardian of the values of the spirit, as protectress of the mortality of the young, she preserves culture, which deals with purposes and ends, while man upholds civilization, which deals only with means."[10]

Archbishop Sheen's insight becomes all the more interesting when we consider again that the height of European culture is related to the heights of Marian devotion. Mary shows herself to be a true mother, even working through culture in ways similar to earthly mothers.

Although this is mentioned in chapter 11, it is well worth repeating that as Mary transforms us, she *does not* make us into a carbon copy of any saint of old; she makes us even more the person we know ourselves to be, but better. There is a mistaken view that holiness is formulaic or boxes one in, but this myth is shattered by looking at the lives of the saints. There is a uniqueness to each saint that knows no equal among men steeped in sin. Marian devotion calls individual persons "to become who God already knows them to be—to become who they already are."[11]

Mary also works through our imperfections. St. Maximilian Kolbe assures us that "the Immaculate knows everything

---

10   Ibid., 188–89.
11   Johann G. Roten, "Marian Devotion for the New Millennium," *Marian Studies* 51 (2000): 86, http://ecommons.udayton.edu/marian_studies/vol51/iss1/7.

and directs everything, on condition that we let ourselves be guided perfectly by her."[12] With the smallness of our child-like trust, she can do great things. She can even work with our weaknesses and repeated sins: "Every fall, even if it be very grave and repeated, serves us always and only as a little step towards a higher perfection." Such falls, he adds, Our Lady permits "in order to heal us of our self-love, our pride, in order to lead us to humility and render us in this way more docile to divine graces."[13] Mary knows our weaknesses but also how to correct them.

Many years ago, there was a very wise priest who was advising a couple that were living together, although they were both still married to their respective spouses. This couple was eager to reconcile themselves to the Faith but felt frozen in their situation. The wise priest told the couple to (1) consecrate themselves to Mary and wear a Miraculous Medal as a sign of their consecration, (2) attend Mass every Sunday and Holy Day of Obligation without receiving the Eucharist, and (3) say a daily Rosary together. Within a year, every obstacle that they had faced to being married to each other and in accord with the teaching of the Catholic faith vanished. While they were clearly doing many great things, as Bishop Hugh Doyle quipped, "no one can live continually in sin and continue to say the rosary: either they will give up sin or they will give up the rosary."[14] This couple persevered

---

12 Kolbe, *Let Yourself Be Led*, loc. 34.
13 Ibid., loc. 52.
14 "The Holy Rosary," *EWTN*, http://ewtn.com/Devotionals/prayers/rosary.

and was greatly rewarded for their obedience and devotion to Mary.

In the end, our holiness "consists, not in extraordinary actions, but in accomplishing well your duties towards God, yourself, and others."[15] It can often be tempting to think that we have to do great things to change the world, but it is truly the small things—praying the Rosary one bead at a time, showing kindness to those we love and mercy to those we don't, being patient and kind when it seems to matter little—that do the most.

Another way that Mary can lead us is through the example of her life. Though little of her life is chronicled in Scripture, much can be gleaned from those few words, and even more can be uncovered while meditating on her role in Christ's life. Above all, however, is the example of her fiat and her willingness through great love to endure all that God asked of her.

Meeting the Real Mary

Despite all the theology, definitions, and distinctions about who Mary is, St. Maximilian reminds us that above all, she is best known through prayer, humility, and love found in everyday life: "Approaching directly, to her heart, you will attain a greater knowledge of her and be inflamed by a greater love for her than all human words together could teach you."[16]

---

15   Kolbe, *Let Yourself Be Led*, loc. 49.
16   Ibid., loc. 60.

In light of this, as Pope Paul VI said of Mary, "we have good reason to place our trust in her in the midst of this terrible disorder."[17] We simply need to allow ourselves to be led by her gentle guidance in confidence and peace, as St. Maximilian Kolbe wrote so long ago: "Let us let ourselves be led, then; let us be *peaceful, peaceful*; let us not attempt to do *more* than that which she wills or *more quickly*. Let us let ourselves be carried by her; she will think of everything and take care of all our needs, of the soul and of the body. Let us give every difficulty, every sorrow to her, and have confidence that she will take care of it better than we could. *Peace*, then, *peace*, much *peace in an unlimited* confidence in her."[18]

---

17   Pope Paul VI, *Christi Matri*, September 15, 1966, #8, *The Holy See*, http://w2.vatican.va/content/paul-vi/en/encyclicals/documents/hf_p-vi_enc_15091966_christi-matri.html.

18   Kolbe, *Let Yourself Be Led*, loc. 348.

CHAPTER 13

Case Study on Pope St. John Paul II

Throughout this book, we have seen Our Lady perform the miraculous, the wonderful, the beautiful. For many, however, it might be difficult to see how she works in our lives in the contemporary world. Yes, we can imagine these things happening long ago, but it isn't so easy to see how she can work today in our dramatically secular culture.

For those still questioning what the Marian Option looks like in a concrete and tangible reality, the life of Pope St. John Paul II offers a perfect example. No stranger to religious persecution under both the Nazis and the Communists—as well as civilizational collapse—his life can serve as a practical field guide for life when your faith is threatened. It is difficult to find a soul devoted to Mary to such an incredible degree.

Pope John Paul hailed from a country that felt the lash of invaders like the bloodthirsty Tartars and Turks, lived through the merciless claw of atheistic National Socialism (the Nazis), and endured the jackboot of Soviet Communism. Poland has been at the front of virtually every major type of ideological battle. Polish people have few illusions about the evil and depravity of which human nature is capable.

Given Poland's history, Marian devotion was tightly woven into the culture when Wojtyła was born. This culture, his parent's devotion, and the close proximity of his home to the local parish—right next door—would all contribute to his ingrained devotion to Our Lady. The Church of the Presentation of Mary was where Wojtyła received his early sacraments, but it was also where he served as an altar boy and where he would frequently stop in to say a prayer at Our Lady's side chapel. The Rosary was also one of the Wojtyła family's regular devotions.

When he was nine years old, Wojtyła's own mother, Emilia, died, leaving a gaping hole in his life that was certainly filled in some way by his spiritual Mother. A year later, Wojtyła was given his first brown scapular, which he wore throughout his life. After being shot on May 13, 1981, he asked the doctors to not remove it while he was in surgery.

After the start of World War II, Wojtyła was introduced to Jan Tyranowski, a tailor-cum-mystic who mentored the young men of the neighborhood parish, St. Stanislaw Kostka, in a group called "The Living Rosary." Composed of fifteen young men, each took a mystery of the Rosary to pray and meditate on. It was through Tyranowski's influence that Wojtyła's appreciation for the Rosary deepened and matured, and he found in it a place of freedom at a time when daily life was anything but free:

> The tailor Tyranowski introduced the young Wojtyła
> to the works of mysticism at a time when the Nazi lie

raged over Europe with calculated precision and the
Russian lash had already begun to strike Poland. In
the young men who listened to him, Tyranowski laid the
mystical foundation for the house of freedom. With
the help of great mystics such as St. John of the Cross
and St. Louis Grignon de Montfort, he taught them
to win their freedom through a daily labor that did not
mark the price . . . In Christ, they found the "living
water" that quenched their desire for the reality that
is the farthest away and at the same time the closest
to man.[1]

Through the dark night of Nazi occupation, Wojtyła found
the deep spiritual vein to Christ, offering peace, hope, and
truth. Grygiel reports that "from the experience of history,
Cardinal Karol Wojtyła and then John Paul II learned that
when man entrusts himself to the consequences of the truth,
he becomes unbreakable. The nation is unbreakable that has
people who wait with courage for the victory of truth."[2]
Notice that Grygiel doesn't say the entire population but
people who wait with courage. The courageous—those who
make up the creative minority—are generally a small lot.

Later, as pope, John Paul II described the impact that
reading St. Louis de Montfort's book *True Devotion to Mary*
had on his life. He said, "The reading of this book was a
decisive turning-point in my life. I say 'turning-point,' but
in fact it was a long inner journey . . . This 'perfect devotion'

---

1   Stanisław Grygiel, *Discovering the Human Person* (Grand Rapids,
     MI: Eerdmans, 2014), 6–7.
2   Ibid., 16.

is indispensable to anyone who means to give himself without reserve to Christ and to the work of redemption. It is from Montfort that I have taken my motto 'Totus tuus' ['I am all yours']."[3]

Through this new world opened up by Tyranowski and the saints, Wojtyła became like clay for Mary to fashion in response to the world's needs—particularly to the fight against Communism.

As pope, John Paul II offered his entire pontificate to her, entrusting everything to her. He found many ways to express his devotion to Our Lady. An *M* appeared on his papal coat of arms, symbolizing Mary, and he frankly admitted that the Rosary was his favorite prayer, both because of the complete picture it paints of Christ's life and because as a simple prayer, it "marks the rhythm of human life."[4] Even in his scholarly work, each encyclical he wrote always ended with a short prayer to the Virgin Mother.

Wojtyła's Tactics in the Face of Religious Persecution

A survey of Pope John Paul II's life reveals that he left the world something of a field guide to combat religious persecution and civilizational rot. He faced persecution first under the Nazi's deadly form of social engineering, which involved erasing the Jews and Poles from the Third Reich. Through a

---

3   Quoted in St. Louis de Montfort, *True Devotion to Mary* (Charlotte, NC: TAN Books, 2010), vi.

4   Pope John Paul II, *Rosarium Virginis Mariae*, October 2, 2016, #25, *The Holy See*, https://w2.vatican.va/content/john-paul-ii/en/apost_letters/2002/documents/hf_jp-ii_apl_20021016_rosarium-virginis-mariae.html.

combination of determination, humor, prudence, and faith, he not only survived the war but also aided others, including many Jews. Then under Soviet Communism, Wojtyła rose through the episcopal ranks, eventually becoming the second most powerful prelate in Poland. Cunning, patience, adaptation, and again (as always) faithfulness helped him as the Bishop of Krakow and later as Pope John Paul II, the Bishop of Rome, chip away at Communism and remind those behind the Iron Curtain the truth about themselves: they were made to love and serve God, not the Soviet machine.

Throughout the trials, Wojtyła didn't retreat (although he did attempt a type of retreat in a failed effort to join the Carmelites) but served the Church dramatically through Our Lady's guidance. John Paul II offers a prime example of one living the Marian Option and evidence that Mary will help us live out our unique mission. Here are eight of his tools.

Be Not Afraid

John Paul started his pontificate urging the world: "Do not be afraid." It is not merely a cute phrase; having lived through both Nazi oppression and Soviet Communism, he knew what it was to be afraid. This phrase, the most frequent line in Scripture, was a recurrent theme throughout his twenty-six years as pope. From his own experience, he knew that fear could be paralyzing. In dealing with it, Pope John Paul II offered this insight: "Fear decreases when love increases." Often fear chokes us and leaves us feeling isolated. At the heart of John Paul's insight is the necessity of thinking of *someone* else—that is, loving only yourself isn't going to rid you of fear. Love moves us beyond ourselves to the needs of others—sometimes even the needs of our enemies—freeing us from fear.

Before becoming Pope Francis, Archbishop Bergoglio said at John Paul II's beatification Mass, "John Paul II had no fear, this is precisely why he combated dictatorships. Pope Wojtyła had no fear because he lived his life in contemplation of the Risen Lord."[5] Here again, the focus is not on ourselves but on Someone else.

John Paul's pontificate was focused on freeing people from fear. It was this that made his papacy so powerful, as the Soviets would soon find out.

Learn the Enemies' Tactics and Adapt

Rather than making a sea of public martyrs (though hundreds of thousands of private ones were made in the gulags), the Communists employed other tactics to control the masses, including intimidation, arrests, violence, and surveillance. They were also masters of media manipulation. During John Paul's first visit to Poland in 1979, the cameramen were told to only take tight shots of the pope to hide the swelling numbers from view. Any footage of the crowd was only to include clergy, nuns, and the elderly and handicapped.

Instead of throwing his hands up in frustration with the enemies' tactics, John Paul was able to find new ways to confound the enemy by doing the unexpected. When he realized

---

5   Vatican Insider Staff, "Francis: 'Wojtyła, the Fearless Pope,'" *La Stampa*, April 2, 2013, http://www.lastampa.it/2013/04/02/vaticaninsider/eng/the-vatican/francis-Wojtyła-the-fearless-pope-NHye7YXwaN0fD0iAiFE0WO/pagina.html.

the archbishop's residence was bugged, he held important meetings outside. He spoke loudly inside about things he wanted the Communists to hear. When he was followed on the way to a secret meeting, his driver stealthily dropped him off at another waiting car without being detected by those on his tail.

The Communists made every effort to keep people apart and drive a wedge between the most intimate of relationships. To combat this, Wojtyła encouraged married couples to renew their wedding vows, he created opportunities for young people to congregate together in the countryside, and he never showed any outward sign other than absolute accord with the Primate of Poland, Cardinal Wyszyński, so the bishops could not be played against each other. He was the embodiment of being shrewd as a serpent but innocent as a dove (Mt 10:16).

Be Mindful of Who You Are and Who God Is

Wojtyła noticed early on that the Communist oppressors manipulated people by taking away their dignity, their self-respect, and their identity as willed and loved by God. Every effort was made to strip the culture of its Catholic identity.

As archbishop of Krakow and pope, John Paul II made heroic efforts to proclaim the truth of Christ. When the Communists built the "model town" of Nowa Huta without a church (unheard of in Poland), the Archbishop of Krakow spent twenty years in direct resistance to the state, coordinating countless volunteers and laborers to finally build a church. He was vigilant in reminding particularly the Poles—and the rest of the world—that they were more than who the Communists said they were. This was the first strike in bringing down the Berlin wall ten years later.

Keep a Sense of Humor

One biographer tells the tale that when dealing with the Gestapo during World War II, Wojtyła would periodically don a disguise as a German soldier—complete with a German accent—in a perilous effort to help the Jews. Trying to sew discord among the soldiers, Wojtyła and his friends, also in disguise, issued a directive to the German troops that all cats in Krakow were to be registered. While Wojtyła's mission was carried out with seriousness because of the deadly stakes, one can imagine the laughter as Wojtyła and his friends came up with the scheme.

Years later, after becoming pope and at the end of his first tense visit to Poland, John Paul planted a kiss on the cheek of Henryk Jabłoński on international television, much to the Socialist leader's embarrassment. And on a state visit to the United States, after lunch at the Cathedral Rectory in Washington, DC, John Paul II slid down the banister of a set of backstairs into the arms of a shocked Secret Service agent. The agent just stood there, stunned, unable to figure out what to do. The pope laughingly wagged his finger at the agent and scoffed, "Secret Service," as if to say, "You guys will have your hands full with me!" John Paul was a man who clearly valued humor.

Be Vigilant and Hopeful

Being vigilant was a recurring theme imparted on John Paul's trips to Poland, especially to young people. The political "dance" between the Poles—led by Lech Wałęsa of the solidarity movement—and the Communist government suffered many setbacks and disappointments, among them the imposition of martial law and the violent murder of Father Jerzy Popiełuszko.

And yet, as Cardinal Stanisław Dziwisz recounts in his book *A Life With Karol*, part of the genius of Karol Wojtyła was that he never gave in to pessimism: "He would always say, 'Christ is in the Church.' In other words, there would be calm after the storm. There would a springtime after the winter."[6] And even when things looked terrible, Wojtyła's approach was to "salvage what could be salvaged."[7]

Pray

This one seems obvious, but what is not so evident is the abundance of peace, insight, and inner freedom that prayer gave to John Paul. We normally look to prayer to change the external realities of our life, but the Polish pope also knew the power of prayer could change the internal. Like the sinking Peter, who panicked when he saw a storm while walking on water, Christ reached out to grab him instead of calming the storm. In other words, Christ did not make the storm go away but instead came straight to Peter to pull him back up, just like He can vivify our hearts with His grace without actually taking away our crosses; the grace simply helps us carry the cross.

---

6   Stanisław Dziwisz, *Life With Karol* (New York: Double Day, 2008), 201–2.
7   Ibid., 47.

Prayer is also vitally important for answering big questions, such as "What should my vocation be?" or "Should I move my family near a monastery?" One novice master at a monastery once said to me, "Some join the monastery for the wrong reason." Some are called to one place, others are called to something quite different, but we must have "spiritual ears" to hear the call—ears that are only formed through prayer.

Remember That God Can Work Through the Enemies' Vices
Father Wojtyła was assigned to St. Florian's Church in Krakow, which had an outreach to the local universities. This outreach was vastly complicated by Communism. In Communist Poland, few could be trusted, and any public activity was dangerous, so trying to provide religious culture to young people where the secular "culture" was toxic was a daunting task. But even this seemingly desolate ground—where normal public activity was highly discouraged and sometimes illegal and Communist ideology poisoned everything—proved to be fruitful for those who loved God.

Because they had to hide their activities from the Communists, the members of Wojtyła's group—and the Church in general—were compelled into living in strictly personal relations. "Thanks also to this dynamic," Wlodzimierz Redzioch, a colleague of the pope, explained, "in that semi-clandestine state, the relations of friendship and mutual trust became stronger and stronger and revealed to us the beauty of the Church, which made us free from everything that is bound up with mere ownership. Thus God made use of and still makes use of those who deny him."[8] Even out of great darkness can come a great light.

Build Real Culture

Wlodzimierz Redzioch explained that culture, as Wojtyła understood it, is related to cultivation and raising of crops of maturing souls: "John Paul II saw how culture consists of knowing how to cultivate the earth on which man grows and matures 'so as to rise again,' to use the expression of the great polish poet C. K. Norwid."[9] He continued, "Culture cannot be reduced to learning. On the contrary, nothing is more dangerous to society than learned men who are without culture. Because only culture is life-giving, because the purpose of culture is 'to rise again.' Culture is either paschal or it is not culture."[10]

This overlaps one of the arguments for the Benedict Option (one of the most compelling, in fact): creating a free space for families to raise and educate children and construct culture is how civilization is renewed and extended.

Changing the Course of History

Each of these eight tactics played some role in Wojtyła's formation of others in Krakow and in his pontificate. They contributed to his role in bringing down Soviet Communism without massive bloodshed—something no one expected

---

8   Wlodzimierz Redzioch, ed., *Stories About Saint John Paul II* (San Francisco: Ignatius Press, 2015), 62.

9   Ibid., 60.

10   Ibid., 61.

given Soviet bellicosity, the massive thirty-year arms race between the Soviets and the United States, and the significant stakes involved.

But no story of Pope John Paul II and his devotion to Our Lady would be complete without mention of the 1981 assassination attempt on his life. On May 13, 1981, the Feast of Our Lady of Fatima, several shots were fired at the Holy Father by Mehmet Ali Ağca, a hired assassin, in St. Peter's Square. Years later, when John Paul met with Ali Ağca in prison, Ali Ağca expressed his amazement that the pope did not die. "So why aren't you dead?" was the first thing he said to the pope.[11] He was sure of his target. It was later reported that as John Paul was shot, he made a slight movement toward a little girl with a holy card of Our Lady of Fatima, offsetting Ali Ağca's target. Father Donald Calloway wrote, "Our Lady of Fatima saved him on that day, and he knew it."[12] As the pope himself would say, "One hand pulled the trigger, another hand guided the bullet."[13]

While still recovering at the hospital, Pope John Paul II asked that the third part of the Fatima Secret be brought to him to read once more. As we saw before, that section of the secret said a bishop dressed in white would be killed. John Paul knew he was the bishop, but he also knew that his life had been spared. As Cardinal Dziwisz speculated, perhaps the whole point of the third part of the secret was to show

11   Dziwisz, *Life With Karol*, 137.
12   Donald Calloway, *Champions of the Rosary* (Stockbridge: MA, Marian Press, 2016), 317.
13   Dziwisz, *Life With Karol*, 136.

man that events could be changed through prayer: "Couldn't it have been trying to tell us that the paths of history, of human existence, are not necessarily fixed in advance? And that there is a Providence, a 'motherly hand,' which can intervene and cause a shooter, who is certain of hitting his target to miss?"[14]

14 Ibid.

CHAPTER 14

The Marian Solution

There is a contemporary joke about a man whose house is flooding, but he is confident that God will save him. As the water rises, a farmer in a truck comes by to offer him a ride to higher ground. "Oh, no, the Lord will save me!" the man says confidently. Next, as the water rises to the first floor of his home, a rescuer in a boat comes by to help. "Oh, no, the Lord will save me!" he says, again refusing help. Finally, perched on his roof because the water has nearly covered his entire home, a helicopter comes by to pluck him off the shingles. "Oh, no, the Lord will save me!" he shouts again through the torrential wind and rain. And then the man is washed away by the current and drowns. At his arrival at the pearly gates, the man says to God, "Why didn't you save me?" And God says, "I tried. I sent a truck, a boat, and a helicopter."

Looking back on Marian history, we look a bit like this man. Over and over again, in every age, in every country, Mary has tried to help us. She has offered us material life-savers—through the brown scapular and the Miraculous

Medal—and a myriad of spiritual vehicles to find the way home to her Son. Mary has made it clear that she loves us and wants to save us, and she has given us the tools to be saved through the grace of her Son. What more can she possibly do to show her love for humanity?

Blessed Alan de la Roche reports that Jesus said to him, "If only these poor wretched sinners would say My Rosary, they would share in the Merits of My Passion and I would be their Advocate and would appease My Father's Justice."[1] What he meant was that the problems of the world would dissolve so quickly—sinners would be converted, wars would be stopped, diseases would be eradicated, and life would have an order, creativity, and harmony beyond our imagining today. One can almost imagine an annoyed Jesus, throwing His hands up in the air as He sighs, "If only they would pray the Rosary!" But as He made clear to Blessed Alan, the Rosary isn't just Mary's gift, it is *His* Rosary too. It is about His life, His sacrifice, His suffering, and His desire to unite us with His Father.

At the beginning of this book, we looked at the Marian Option through the lens of "how to deal with civilization decay as well as Christian persecution." The chapters that followed have argued that more than any saint or noble leader, Mary offers humanity the surest way to heaven; the best way to cultivate a more heavenly earth is by adhering to her. Not only does she have the desire to help us; she has the ability. The Marian Option in its simplicity can be universally

---

1   St. Louis de Montfort, *The Secrets of the Rosary* (Charlotte, NC: TAN Books, 1993), Twenty-Seventh Rose.

applied to all Catholics, even if particular individuals are called to live other types of options. These other options will only be enhanced by devotion to Mary, not diluted.

What has also become clear in these pages is that, in characteristic Marian form, the Marian Option doesn't just mean one thing; it means more than just picking one avenue to battling culture wars. The Marian Option is something that every man and woman must choose and decide to emulate. We must decide when faced with the true reality of who Mary is whether we will embrace or reject her love. The saints have reported that Satan and all his fallen angels rejected God because of the role that Mary, as a human woman, was to play in salvation history. We must decide if we will go the way of Satan—and so many others who have trampled on her gifts—and reject her. Or we can allow her to love us; to give us peace, joy, and all the virtues; and most important, to bring us to her Son. Mary is the gate of heaven, and we must decide if we will follow her. This is the calling God has willed for us—we are called to "become like little children" (Mt 18:3). Every child naturally runs to his or her mother.

The benefits of choosing Mary go well beyond our own soul and spread out dramatically into the world. Mary shows us how the "yes" of one person can change all of history. We know from the historian Toynbee that it doesn't take many people to change the world. Your "yes" might mean more to the world than you will ever realize this side of heaven.

In opting for Mary, we allow her to become *the Marian Solution*. Like when she asked Jesus to turn water into wine at Cana, she has the ability to help us transform our lives, our families, and our world—one prayer at a time. Our work is to ask and to trust.

And when in doubt, remember the words of St. Bernard: "In danger, in trials, in doubts, think of Mary and cry out to her. Following her, you will never lose your way. Calling out to her, you will never despair."[2]

Ad majorem Dei Gloriam Virginisque
Deiparare, Matris nostrae!

2　　Quoted in St. Alphonsus de' Liguori, "The Glories of Mary," ch. 2, sec. 2, *Devotion to Our Lady*, http://devotiontoourlady .com/the-glories-of-mary-st-alphonsus-liguori.html.

APPENDIX

Daily Ways to Live the Marian Option

There are several ways to draw closer to Our Lady and help transform the world through one small act of love at a time. Here are just a few.

Pray the Rosary

As we saw in chapter 11, the daily Rosary of five to twenty decades is essential.

Here are a few ideas to help you get to it every day.

Keep Rosaries Close

If you have rosaries around, you are more likely to remember to pray it or at least be mindful of Mary.

Listen to the Rosary

When I have a hard time going to sleep, I put on Mother Angelica and her nuns praying the Rosary on my iPad. It always works (particularly the Glorious Mysteries, which seem to be the most soothing of all the recordings). Many versions of the Rosary are also available on CD.

Encourage Others to Pray the Rosary

Praying the Rosary can be daunting to the uninitiated, or it simply doesn't occur to others to pray it. Inviting friends and family to pray it in a group setting (and not putting them on the spot to lead a decade) is a great way to get it on their radar again. You can also pray that others start to pray the Rosary.

Consecrate Yourself to Mary

Marian consecration, particularly through the method of St. Louis de Montfort, is another essential of the Marian Option, one that can be renewed annually.

My family and I consecrate ourselves anew to Mary every January 1 as we begin the New Year. It is nothing elaborate, but we gather in front of a sixteenth-century icon of Mary at our parish. My husband offers a prayer for us to Our Lady and then we pray a Hail Mary. It has become a treasured tradition of our family.

Go to Mass

Every proper Marian devotion leads us to put Christ at the center of our lives. There is no better way to do that than going to Mass.

Find a Holy League (or Establish Your Own)

The Holy League was the name of the soldiers, laity, clergy, and bishops that Pope Pius V united in anticipation of the battle of Lepanto. These holy men prayed the Rosary for victory, knowing that they were completely outnumbered by the Ottomans and that victory would only come through Our Lady's intercession. A new Holy League has cropped up recently at different parishes around the country.

Fill Your Home With Beautiful Marian Artwork

There is an abundance of Marian art available in every style imaginable, from icons to more contemporary art forms. It's also a blessing for children to have icons and other beautiful Marian images in their rooms.

Have Your Home Blessed

This is always a good idea, no matter what the circumstances. Holy water and other sacramentals, like blessed salt, are good to have on hand too.

Go to Adoration/Pray in a Church

If prayer is talking to God, then adoration is one of the supreme forms, with little distraction. Mystagogy, or the science of bringing us to Christ and Christ to us, is at the heart of Mary's work. Adoring Christ makes this work much, much easier. Let her lead you to Him.

If you cannot make it to adoration or a church, simply seek out silence. Our world is full of noise, but we know God speaks to us in a still, small voice (1 Kgs 19:12). Only in silence can this be heard.

Pray the Liturgy of the Hours

These prayers (also known as the Divine Office) are based on the psalms of the Old Testament. They are among the prayers that Mary prayed. The Rosary itself was based on a simplified version of the Divine Office and was known by many as Mary's psalter.

Visit a Marian Shrine

Marian shrines are everywhere. Find the closest one and make a pilgrimage or retreat there.

Pray a Novena to Our Lady Undoer of Knots

Heavily promoted by Pope Francis, this more than three-hundred-year-old devotion originated in Augsburg, Germany, at the church of St. Peter am Perlach. Father Bergoglio learned of the devotion while studying in Germany and has since promoted it in Latin America and now to the universal Church.

Use Mother Theresa's Flying Novena

Mother Teresa used this tool when she needed a prayer answered immediately. It consists of nine Memorares of petition and a tenth for thanksgiving.

Pray the Angelus

Although the pattern of praying three Hail Marys at certain times of the day is an old tradition, the Angelus as we know it today—as a repetition of the meeting between St. Gabriel and Mary at the Annunciation three times a day—dates to the 1500s. It is a prayer for the safety of Christendom and has been used particularly in times of great need to ask for Our Lady's protection. The bell at the noon hour for the Angelus used to be called the "peace bell" in honor of the prayer's petition.

Wear the Brown Scapular

Under the title of Our Lady of Mount Carmel, the modified version of the Carmelite habit was given to St. Simon Stock on July 16, 1251, with the promise that "whoever dies in this garment shall not suffer eternal fire." The scapular is still held up today as a sign of true devotion to Mary, signifying veneration, confidence, and love.

Our Lady said to St. Dominic, "One day by the Rosary and the Scapular, I will save the world."

Wear the Miraculous Medal

Given to St. Catherine Labouré, this medal, as the name implies, has countless miracles associated with it. The first casting of it was twenty-two thousand pieces, which quickly sold out. Within a year, two million had been cast and sold. There is no telling how many worldwide have been cast to date.

Be Mindful of Mary's Constant Presence

St. Maximilian Kolbe has made Marian devotion so much easier through tangible ways to connect with her. Here is one of his best: "It is not a matter here of kneeling down a long time and praying, but of this relationship of a child to its mother. A loving glance at her statue, the frequent repetition of the name *Mary*, even if it be just in our hearts. Different prayers and formulas are good and beautiful, but the essential thing is the simple relationship of a child to its mother, this sense of our need for this mother, the conviction that without her we can do nothing."[1]

---

1   Maximilian Kolbe, *Let Yourself Be Led by the Immaculate* (Kansas City: Angelus Press, 2013), Kindle ed., loc. 67.

Learn the Fatima Prayer

Before Our Lady appeared to the three children at Fatima, an angel appeared on several occasions to help teach the children to pray in preparation for Mary's arrival. The angel taught them this prayer: "My God, I believe, I adore, I hope and I love You! I ask pardon of You for those who do not believe, do not adore, do not hope and do not love You." After he taught it to them, he said, "Pray thus. The Hearts of Jesus and Mary are attentive to the voice of your supplications."[2] Clearly, it is a powerful prayer in reparation for the many offenses in the world today.

Follow First Saturday Devotions of Fatima

At Fatima, Mary requested that on the first Saturday of five consecutive months, we pray to make reparation for the offenses and blasphemies against the Immaculate Heart of Mary. This includes going to confession, receiving Communion, saying five decades of the Rosary, and keeping Mary company for fifteen minutes while meditating on the mysteries of the Rosary.

Put a Statue of Mary Outside Your Home

A statue of Our Lady outside your home is a great reminder of her loving, peaceful, and powerful presence. You can beautify her year round with flowers and by crowning her in May.

Pray for the Souls in Purgatory

The souls in purgatory, we are told by the saints, need our prayers to help them get to heaven. Although they can

---

2   Andrew Apostoli, *Fatima for Today* (San Francisco: Ignatius Press, 2010), 23.

pray for us on earth while still in purgatory, their prayers become more powerful once they are united with God in heaven.

Suggestions Specifically for Families
In addition to the previous list items (many of which can be applied to families), there are many things parents can include in the daily rhythm of life.

Pray the Rosary as a Family
Pope St. John Paul II made this recommendation: "The family that prays together stays together. The holy rosary, by age old tradition, has shown itself particularly effective as a prayer that brings the family together. Individual family members, in turning their eyes toward Jesus, also regain the ability to look one another in the eye, to communicate, to show solidarity, to forgive one another and to see their covenant of love renewed in the Spirit of God."[3]

My own family prays a daily Rosary before bedtime. It took us a while to figure out what works. We have low expectations for the littlest children, while we give the other children more responsibility. Yes, there are times when it is messy or painful, but I know the blessings are still coming to our family and the world through our efforts. My children know well now that if ever they are in trouble, they are to turn to Mary and the Rosary.

---

3   Pope John Paul II, "Rosarium Virginis Mariae" (apostolic letter, October 16, 2002), *The Holy See*, https://w2.vatican .va/content/john-paul-ii/en/apost_letters/2002/documents/ hf_jp-ii_apl_20021016_rosarium-virginis-mariae.html.

Teach Your Children Marian Hymns

Kids love to sing, and there are plenty of simple and beautiful Marian hymns. We usually sing one after the Rosary, but during the Easter season and on feast days, my children love to sing the "Regina Caeli." We taught them the Latin version, so they have no idea what it really means, but they love it particularly because they know it's associated with great feasts.

Say a Hail Mary When You Hear Sirens

This was something a dear woman taught my brother and I when we were quite young. Years later, we both realized that we still did it. Mrs. Meier made quite the impression on us. I do it with my children now, and oftentimes, they will be the ones to suggest it even before I do. It is a great habit to have.

Celebrate Marian Feasts

It's great to find traditions for your family and friends to celebrate Marian feasts in a special way, such as with Mass and a favorite meal or dessert. You could, for example, make star cookies for Mary on the Feast of the Queenship of Mary (Aug. 22) in honor of the "woman clothed with the sun, the moon at her feet, and on her head a crown of twelve stars" (Rv 12:1); make a birthday cake for Mary on the feast of her nativity (Sept. 8); or serve white food (pork, potatoes, cauliflower, and angel food cake) on the Feast of the Immaculate Conception (Dec. 8).[4]

---

4   These ideas come from Margaret Bereit's blog, http://margaret bereit.com.

Tell Stories of Miracles

When I was a little girl, there were two religious sisters—Sister Cecelia and Sister Adelaide—who generously allowed my three siblings and I to stay with them overnight to give my parents a break. I recall praying the Rosary with them in their chapel and then talking late into the night about Marian miracles and those of the angels. There are few things I can point to from my childhood that made more of an impression on my faith than these incredible stories. I see it now with my own children—how wonder is ignited.

Plant a Mary Garden

There are so many flowers and plants named after Mary that huge gardens have been planted in her honor. This can be done on a grand scale with kids, even if it is a small patch in your yard or just a few potted plants in your home.

Use Books, Coloring Books, and DVDs

There is a wealth of books available for children about Mary for every age group. Our favorite is the beautifully illustrated *Take It to the Queen* by Josephine Nobisso (author) and Katalin Szegedi (illustrator). There are also abundant coloring books and DVDs available that are focused on the Rosary or Marian apparitions.

Make Your Own Rosaries

I am not remotely crafty, but after repeatedly fixing our broken rosaries, I realized making them wasn't too tough. My children have loved picking out the beads, crucifixes, and medals for their own rosaries. I made one for a five-year-old girl who was concerned that there was no bead for the Glory Be, so I included extra Glory-Be beads.

For children who are too small to manage beading, rosaries can be made out of painted pasta, beans, or candy. The selected pieces can be glued onto a large poster board, allowing the child to choose the colors and shapes for each decade. This is a fun activity for the Feast of Our Lady of the Rosary.[5]

---

5   Ibid.

FURTHER READING

Apostoli, Andrew. *Fatima for Today*. Ignatius Press, 2010.

Calloway, Donald. *Champions of the Rosary*. Marian Press, 2016.

Cruz, Joan Carroll. *See How She Loves Us*. TAN Books, 2012.

de Montfort, Louis. *True Devotion to Mary*. TAN Books. 2010.

Gorny, Grzegorz, and Janusz Rosikon. *Guadalupe Mysteries: Deciphering the Code*. Ignatius Press, 2016.

Klein, Judy. *Mary's Way: The Power of Entrusting Your Child to God*. Ave Maria Press, 2016.

Sheen, Fulton J. *The World's First Love*. Ignatius Press, 2010.

Thigpen, Paul. *A Year With Mary*. TAN Books, 2015.

Warner, Christopher B. *Rule of the Mother of God: The Eastern Rosary of Saint Seraphim*. Christopher Warner, 2009.

ACKNOWLEDGMENTS

The spark for this book came from a lecture I first gave at the Acton Institute's annual Acton University. I would like to thank all my friends there for the encouragement and keen insights, especially Michael and Rebecca Matheson Miller, David Clayton, and Patrice and Christopher Warner.

I am also grateful for the great folks at TAN Books and their faith in this project, particularly Conor Gallagher, Rick Rotondi, John Moorehouse, and Brian Kennelly. Any errors in this book are their fault (just kidding). Special thanks to Brian for his steady editing, which helped take this book to eleven.

I also need to extend my thanks to the Norbertine Canonnesses of the Bethlehem Priory of St. Joseph for their powerful prayer support and to Father Jeffry Kirby for his friendship and assistance.

I remain forever indebted to my husband, Joseph, for his patience, inspiration, wisdom, and ability to cook while tending to four children. This book would have remained a mustard seed without his support and hard work.

TAN·BOOKS

TAN Books is the Publisher You Can Trust With Your Faith.

TAN Books was founded in 1967 to preserve the spiritual, intellectual, and liturgical traditions of the Catholic Church. At a critical moment in history TAN kept alive the great classics of the Faith and drew many to the Church. In 2008 TAN was acquired by Saint Benedict Press. Today TAN continues to teach and defend the Faith to a new generation of readers.

TAN publishes more than 600 booklets, Bibles, and books. Popular subject areas include theology and doctrine, prayer and the supernatural, history, biography, and the lives of the saints. TAN's line of educational and homeschooling resources is featured at TANHomeschool.com.

TAN publishes under several imprints, including TAN, Neumann Press, ACS Books, and the Confraternity of the Precious Blood. Sister imprints include Saint Benedict Press, Catholic Courses, and Catholic Scripture Study.

For more information about TAN,
or to request a free catalog, visit
TANBooks.com

Or call us toll-free at
(800) 437-5876